A Year in Pinstripes
...and Then Some

BILLY SAMPLE

DEDICATION

Aunt Wincey Recard took me to my first major league game. The Yankees were hosting the Twins in the summer of 1965, with Whitey Ford throwing against Jim "Mudcat' Grant. At one of our numerous charity events over the years, I told 'Mud' about my first game. Aunt Wincey also makes a tasty dandelion wine ... just sayin'. In the same week, Aunt Edna Hunter took her son Stan, my brother Thomas and me to our first National League game at Shea Stadium.

Cousin Stan on the left, and I ready to play some stoop ball in Brooklyn in the late 1950s. Long before computers, Stan was passionate about playing APBA baseball board games.

Jim Bunning went the distance, surrendering two hits in a 5-1 Phillies victory. Both Mets hits came off the bat of 25-year-old Johnny Lewis. Years later, as the

Cardinals' hitting coach, Johnny smiled as he recalled that day as one of those hits left the yard. I often remind Aunt Bernice Lewis (no relation to Johnny) when money was tight, how much I appreciated those Banlon casual shirts she bought from the Veterans Administration's canteen for the start of my school year. It helped me put a little strut in my step. And Aunt Elnora Parker, along with her daughter Janice, without me asking, became an investor in Reunion 108. It was all about the nephew and the family. Thank you all ...

CONTENTS

ACKNOWLEDGMENTS

Throughout all of the humorous episodes included in the book, I hope that my appreciation for being in such a select profession as baseball comes through in my writings. My friends, family and teammates have added to my appreciation of the skills needed to play baseball at the highest level. Many times I didn't play the game at its highest level. As frustrating as that was, I am still glad for having had the opportunity to fail; if for no other reason than the older I get, the better I was. By the time you finish reading this short book, I'll have convinced you that I was as good as Babe Ruth. As it is, I'm only three degrees away from the Sultan of Swat: Ruth to Dixie Walker to Gaylord Perry to me.

While in college, Debi would drive six hours round-trip by herself to watch a baseball game long before we were married. She still can't tell you what a sacrifice fly is, but she showed up for all of the games, even after we were married and she often had two young children in tow. Those young children, Nikki and Ian, became athletes in their own right. Nikki threw the javelin at the University of Rhode Island and Ian caught 10 of Colt Brennan's NCAA record 58 touchdown passes at the University of Hawaii in 2006. Travis came along later, and has become a fitness guru of some note.

I've gotten a lot of advice on how to write a book. Some of it I welcomed, and some had me begging people not to give their opinions. Some of the advisors currently have new books out, as has longtime friend Brian Barrow with his Jack London-esque book set in 1890s Yukon Territory titled *Midstation*. David Jordan and hard throwing 1970-80s right-hander John D'Acquisto have co-authored a book titled *Stolen Seasons*. Tom Sabellico co-authored a book with Pat O'Brien and former major league pitcher, Jim 'Mudcat' Grant, titled *12 Black Aces*, highlighting African-American pitchers who had 20-win seasons. Author and motivational speaker, Billy Staples has among his books, little known stories about 20 baseball heroes called *Beyond the Glory*. Mary Angelo co-authored a book with my cousin, Larry LeGrande about his days in the Negro Leagues and with the Satchel Paige All-Stars titled *I Found Someone to Play With*. Control artist and 1970 20-game winner Fritz Peterson shared his knowledge of publishing three baseball books, the latest called *When the Yankees Were On the Fritz*. Fritz also introduced me to his cover designer, Tony Ficca and his formatter and consultant Jolea M. Harrison, who is also an author. *King* is the latest science fiction tale in her Guardians of the Word series.

A few years ago with a lot of help I made an irreverent baseball clubhouse comedy, called *Reunion 108*. The movie is currently on Amazon Instant Download and DVD. Many of the financiers have been very patient waiting for a return on their investment. That patience has allowed me the freedom to concentrate on writing *A Year in Pinstripes ... And Then Some*. My heartfelt thanks go out to:

Bryan, Michelle, Tom and Nicole Civitarese, Tom Lewandowski, Karen Kaeumlen, Ian Sample, Elizabeth Burton, Sharon Darak, Tadashi Mitsui, Mike Kouyoumdjian, Thomas Sample, Christine Gunkel, John Hirt, Cynthia Swanson, Glenn and Judy Mekles, Gael Corris, James Suttles, Kenneth Altman, Greg Kraus, Anthony and Stephanie Sample, Colm Cahill, Bob Schaner, Estel Walker, Dave Nieratko, Natalhya Khaykov, Elizabeth Berry and Ayae Hamanaka.

Some of my love of writing emanated from the inspiration of English teachers I had in high school. Teachers like Malinda Sayers, Judy Pitts and Beth Byrd, held my attention as I learned how to create interesting themes. They were all good-looking so holding my attention was not that difficult. I didn't grasp syntax as well as other parts of English composition, and that's where having a top-notch editor like Leigh Moore is a much appreciated requisite.

Entertainment lawyer John J. Tormey III, and Baseball Card Promoter Joe Zaccaro helped fill in the blanks of book production. Photographers Andy Richter, Steve Mack, Percy Ahene, Andrea Joy Nussinow, Brad Newton, Jeffrey Feller, Rich Pilling and Derek Storm added photos or advice. Bob Olen and Louis Requena are no longer with us, but Louie left me with this memory, "Goodnight all of you fine people ... and you too, Billy Sample."

There were too many numbers and statistics to footnote, many of them I knew from memory, but it was extremely helpful to have Baseball Almanac, Wikipedia and especially Baseball-Reference.com as backup for researching numbers and dates.

Big thanks to 1985 teammates Mike Pagliarulo and Andre Robertson, who helped trigger my memories from that eventful season. Eventful in the sense that it seemed something was going on every day. Compared to the Texas Rangers, the Yankees were a bit more guarded as a team, but that is understandable when you consider the whirlwind of activity around New York City.

INTRODUCTION

As a baseball player I often thought of myself as an entertainer. Not necessarily in the same sense as a singer, comedian, dancer or actor, but I could hold your attention. Sometimes I held your attention in a positive way and other times, it was not so positive. For the most part that difference depended on what side of the ledger your partisanship was attached. In the post-baseball careers of broadcasting and writing, my philosophy about using my often unique insight is to enhance your appreciation of the game. In *A Year in Pinstripes ... and Then Some*, I believe I do just that. The book may elicit a 'I wasn't aware of that' or might simply bring out a smile or any number of reactions in between. When that happens, and I'm sure it will, I have done my job. Thank you. Enjoy.

MAKING IT THROUGH THE ICE AGE

The year was 1985, long before iPhones, iPads and whatever else will be new by the time you finish this book. Even cell phones were virtually non-existent. Don't believe me? Watch a movie from that era, and see how phone calls were made. How did we pick up friends and relatives at the airport without a cell phone to check on flights, terminals and/or gates? How did we travel from Point A to Point B without GPSs? And if the cell phone was in its infancy, then microwave ovens and television remote controls were in their early childhoods. Yes, people under thirty years of age, there were volume and channel knobs on the television that we actually had to get up and turn. Now we didn't have as many channels, but manually changing the channel was limiting and it really wasn't that long ago. Ultimately, my intent is not to bore anyone with a history lesson, although I do appreciate knowing how we got to where we are. I'm simply doing some minor scene setting for the mid-1980s.

I played most of my major league career with the Texas Rangers. I was drafted twice under the recommendation of the late, great Joe Branzell, the first totally honest scout I had met up until 1973. Joe's work in the D.C./Baltimore area with youth and the community was legendary. History alert again, this was long before the amateur baseball draft was held on MLB.com or the MLB Network, neither of which existed. Drafted players often found out their draft status a day or two after the draft. I knew I was getting drafted, heck the scouts had told me I was going somewhere in the mid-teens, so I awaited my draft phone call on my senior high school graduation trip to Myrtle Beach, South Carolina.

There were six of us student-athletes sharing one room for a week, arranged by Dave Nave, the shortstop on the school's baseball team. There were three African-Americans and three whites, a distinction I make because I realized after the second day that whenever the blacks entered the swimming pool, the other whites immediately left the water. Charlie Morgan was a black man with very light complexion, so he was the wild card. People didn't leave when he was with the white pals, but when noticeably darker classmates like Carey Casey and me, entered the pool, the exodus was swift, with indignation. Armed with our newfound power, Carey and I would announce later in the week, "Hey, we're going downstairs to clear out the pool!" I did this near gleefully even though I did and continue to have the buoyancy of a rock.

The draft call I waited for came three days into the vacation, "Bill, this is Joe Branzell of the Texas Rangers. The Rangers drafted you in the 28th round."

Silence on my end. I didn't even know they had that many rounds. I was more surprised than disappointed, though only disappointment came through the landline. At the time there were only 24 teams and the next thing I hear is, "Well, Bill, 23 other teams passed over you 27 times!"

Hmm, as if he was saying, 'Don't blame us for drafting you.' That revelation stung until I heard that it wasn't the first time he had used that line. I'm not sure what the offer was, but it couldn't have been much more than a two thousand dollar signing bonus, and that wasn't enough to pay for college. Thus, I was labeled as a 'draft and follow', and went to previously all-female Madison College, which later became James Madison University, to play baseball for a school whose baseball program was all of four years old. This, under the direction of now legendary baseball coach Brad Babcock. Then again, that was the only school that offered me any money for college.

Eligible for the draft after my junior year, I was drafted again by Branzell and the Rangers, this time in the tenth round. In order to enhance my draft status, I was switched from left field to second base during the second half of that season, and though he understood, it wasn't exactly music to the ears of incumbent second baseman Vic Cicchino. My move back into the infield (I was a third baseman in high school) was not a comfortable match, and a few years later, I set the Texas League (Double-A) record for errors by a second baseman, and was switched back to the outfield.

I made three errors in a game, at least three times, and if I see teammate hurler, Hal Kelly anytime in life, an apology is the first thing coming out of my mouth. I cost the Plant City, Florida native a game with yet another throwing error in San Antonio, (I had that psychological block that affected Steve Sax and Chuck Knoblauch), and the first thing Hal did was to console me, especially touching, because he didn't win another game in the subsequent three months of the season. I made so many errors that even when I had an errorless game, they gave me an error. Shortstop, Blair Stouffer, out of the University of Texas, coming off a knee injury, was playing one night with three errors, and botched a double-play grounder.

I immediately went into first baseman mode, stretching for the force, which he threw beyond my reach. I thought to myself, "Yeah I know I suck defensively, but even as bad as I am, I haven't made four errors in a game." Looked in the paper the next day, yep, I was assigned his fourth error, and when one makes miscues in bunches, it's not as though the official scorer is going to change the decision.

In addition to Mr. Kelly, there are at least three other pitchers to whom I owe an apology, but that's for another chapter or another book. Okay, okay, to Jon Matlack for losing Lamar Johnson's liner while battling those low light stanchions in old Arlington Stadium, allowing the second run to score in a 3-0 loss to the Chicago White Sox.

And to Mike Smithson for losing Eddie Murray's bases loaded drive into the equally low light stanchions at old Memorial Stadium in Baltimore, with one of my high school's English teachers, Carl Colley, in attendance with his friends. I was hoping that the ball would hit somewhere on my body so it would stay in front of me. I wasn't within six feet of it.

John Henry Johnson gets an apology for me taking two steps in on a Todd Cruz line drive in Kansas City, the last game before the All-Star break in 1979. Willie Wilson was on first, what were my chances of keeping him from scoring with two outs when the drive went over my head?

And the biggest apology goes to Zane Smith, from a first inning play with two outs and the bases loaded at Wrigley. There is an old sports simile about a monkey and a football; apply it here. As soon as the ball left Gary Matthew's bat and I spun in the opposite direction from my first crossover step in right field, I knew I was in trouble, and decades later, as I wince in remembrance, I still feel that grip of uncertainty.

Oh yeah, can I throw an apology to a non-pitcher in here as well? I almost forgot that error they gave to catcher Joe Russell in Double-A, Jackson, Mississippi, when I failed to cover the bag. Nowadays, the official scorer will go to the clubhouse after the game to find out which middle infielder was supposed to cover on the steal attempt, but not then. Sorry Joe.

Now, you might think making all of these admissions is therapeutic. No, they haunt me like a Stephen King movie, which reminds me that playing the sun in right field of Stephen's favorite yard, Fenway Park, is a nightmare too. During one half-inning, manager Doug Radar, had Larry Parrish and me switch from right field to left. When a left-handed hitter was up to bat, I would go to the pull field in right to battle the sun. Does this come with combat pay? The sunglasses under the bill of my cap were merely decorative. Well, in all fairness, Larry was a converted third baseman learning to play the outfield. Nevertheless, I will still accept the combat pay if offered.

Let me backtrack for a second, I should mention that my ascension towards professional baseball was enhanced by playing in the Shenandoah Valley semi-pro summer league. Some of the best amateur players along the eastern seaboard, spent a hot summer honing their talents in an effort to heighten their draft status. Most often the players were housed with host families and given a food stipend for two meals a day. If you were like me, with no other means of income, then you worked a job during the day before the nighttime contest. I was a painter at my college; well, often I held a brush up against a dorm room wall while snoring from a lack of sleep. Then again, all the sleep in the world wasn't going to help me make solid contact with my first experience with the slider. I held my bat high in the air, and even though I transferred my weight to the front foot earlier than most, I kept my hands back well and could hit fastballs, curves and change-ups. But that slider that looks like a fastball, but breaks at the very last split-second, was a challenge for my stance, and I struggled. I made a couple of adjustments at the plate and stayed out of the slider abyss long enough to stay in the starting lineup on a team that would eventually win the regular season title for the Harrisonburg Turks.

The area lays claim to the Turkey Capital of the World, so, you may insert your own joke here without fear of reprisal. Future major leaguers playing in the league included opponents Tom Brookens, who would pick up a World Series ring with the 1984 Detroit Tigers and Denny Walling, who was absolutely the best amateur player I had ever seen, and subsequently a first round pick of the Oakland A's. Teammates going to the majors included infielder, Jim Pankovitz, pitcher Dave Tobik and low-flying outfielder, Gene Richards, who set a National League record for most stolen bases by a rookie with the San Diego Padres in 1977, stealing 56 in 68 attempts.

As a stand alone, those numbers are very impressive, but even more so when you consider that first year players aren't familiar with individual pitcher's pick-off moves. And if stealing at an 82% success rate doesn't impress you, then try the numbers Tim Raines posted. Tim broke Gene's National League rookie stolen base record by pilfering 71 out of 82 attempts in 1981. An 87% success rate during a season in which he played in 88 of the Expos' 108 games, losing two months' worth of the season due to labor unrest.

Rangers assistant general manager, Joe Klein, wanted to see firsthand, the talent his organization drafted, so he added rookie ball manager to his resume. At one early gathering of the Sarasota Rangers, he told us to take a look to both our left and right, pick out another player from each direction, and including yourself, that is all who will make it to the major leagues. He wasn't saying it so much as a scare tactic, but as a realization of the odds of making it in this highly select profession.

I must have picked Steve Comer, a change-up artist out of the University of Minnesota, who preceded me to the majors, and Brian Allard, who pitched in nineteen games over a three-year period with the Rangers and Mariners, to accompany me to the majors. We shared housing and ballfields at the former, Kansas City Baseball Academy, with the Royals, on the outskirts of Sarasota. Most of us were stuck there for the duration of the two and a half months. Only a few players repeating rookie ball had modes of transportation who would take us into the heart of the city to alleviate our boredom. On a couple of occasions one Royals' outfielder from Venezuela would offer his personal remedy to the boredom, by playing pool in the recreation room, with a part of his anatomy, that for most of us, would need a larger pool stick ... or smaller pool table. He would occasionally miscue, but no one was offering to chalk it for him, thus, he didn't lose his turn.

Under the stewardship of manager, Jose Martinez, the Royals had to be the best conditioned team in this hemisphere. They ran around the four field complex, they ran between the fields, they ran to lunch, they ran to military cadences, they ran sprints in the rain when lightning was bouncing off metal poles, they ran so much I would get exhausted watching them run. At one point before the start of the season after watching their exhausted players continue to run, our steward declared, "I don't believe baseball is a track meet, but we'll see."

The connotative meaning of that sentence was not lost on me, and facing a talented, older (more college player signees) team that had future major leaguer Ken Phelps, we beat them seven out of nine times, and brought home the championship for the Sarasota Rangers. Heck, we ran enough in the morning that it was hard to find energy for the noontime contests, I had no idea where the Royals got their energy. Oh, and yours truly battled through a late season slump to lead the league in hitting with a .382 average. Take that, cardiovascular system.

Minor league managers had a lot to say about the makeup of their respective clubs, and I was the last player chosen by Double-A manager, Marty Martinez. His team was going to Tulsa, the first year for the franchise in Oklahoma, and the first year Tulsa dropped from a Triple-A organization under the Cardinals to the lower 1977 status. Previous to being told of my spring and summer destination, I remember looking wistfully at the Tulsa Drillers' brochure, while listening to the players who knew they were going to Tulsa, talk about their plans for the city, which included the fun times in addition to the baseball playing. I don't know if any of them knew about the strange liquor laws in where you had to bring your own alcohol to the bar, hand it over to the bartender and then have the bartender charge you to set up your own liquor for consumption. Anyway, I digress.

Farm Director (now called Players Personnel Directors) Hal Keller, gave me an opportunity to talk him into allowing me to skip Class A ball (Asheville, North Carolina). Freeman 'Tree' Evans was ahead of me on the depth chart, having a good year the previous season with a co-oped (combined with another organization) team in the Midwest. I told Hal I would go to Tulsa even if I had to DH. Well, they found an outfield spot for Tree, and I played second base. This ended shortly after the All-Star break due to my defensive shortcomings. I batted third in a lineup behind Tree, who stole 51 bags. Leadoff batter, nineteen year old, Ed Miller, stole 80 bases even while missing a month of the season due to an injury. Yep, the fastball hitter saw a lot of fastballs, and the Tulsa Drillers won the first half of the league.

I batted .348 for the season, which was amazing, not because it was second in the league, but because it included an 0 for 37 slump towards the end of the season. I went eleven consecutive games without a hit, and there weren't many hard hit balls in that futility. The eleven consecutive games without a hit cost me a call-up to the majors, as speedy Ed did get the call and was the Rangers only Double-A promotion.

As bad as the 0 for 37 was, and it was bad, it could have been worse. While at James Madison University, I remember having a conversation with Dean Dean Ehlers, (no, that's not a typo, he was the Dean of Athletics and his first name is Dean. Yep, confusing I know) told me about taking an 0 for 42 while playing winter ball in the Dominican Republic. There is no way I can go 0 for that long, right? If not for a day off and a scratch infield single, I could have gone 0 for 55, with a real suicide watch over me.

One of our owners in Tulsa was country music star, Roy Clark, who said he was scouted by the St. Louis Browns in the 1940s, ("yesterday when I was young"). He would occasionally take ground balls on the left side of the infield and didn't look bad doing it; dare I say he could 'pick it'? Okay, there it is, I said it.

Roy was working out with us during the next to last game of the season. The last game of the year didn't affect team standings, so our pitching coach, Frank Bolick, would pitch and the lineup would be a mismatch of uniformed and non-uniformed personnel that included our trainer, Danny Wheat. This is where Roy could play, but he had an out-of-town commitment that he could not break. Somewhere Roy got the signals mixed and was headed to the plate with a bat in his hands on this next to the last game of the season when the game was still serious. The entire team in the dugout acted in unison and grabbed this ballad singing jock and sat his pickin' and grinnin' self down.

The Jackson Mets were throwing Juan Berenguer, who was clocked at 98 m.p.h. on the 'slow' gun. In his Triple-A season the following year, Berenguer had broken a couple of batters' bones, I heard it was a jaw and a wrist, and just for effect, he was trying to pitch me inside, to the extent that I told the Mets' catcher, Stan Hough, that I was getting tired of hitting the dirt during all of Berenguer's starts.

He did throw me a non-knockdown pitch that I'll always remember. It was a first-pitch fastball strike in Jackson, Mississippi, to which I never reacted. I saw the powerful windup, heard a pop in the mitt, and saw the ball go back into the pitcher's glove. I knocked the imaginary dirt off my spikes, as if I was looking for another pitch from someone who threw ninety percent fastballs.

I had one other pitch thrown to me that year that I will also never forget. The setting was Shreveport, Louisiana and Don Robinson of the Shreveport Pirates was on the mound, another pitcher who, like Berenguer, had a very good major league career. I can't remember if the count was 0-2 or 1-2, but I do remember that the two-strike curveball broke with such late, forceful parabola, seemingly inches from my face for strike three, that my knees shook walking back to the dugout.

I was surprised that none of my teammates teased me about my knees shaking as I'm sure everyone could see my unsteady gait. Later in my career I would face young Dennis Martinez' curveball, which was sharp and heavy, as well as Bert Blyleven's signature pitch that you could hear spin as it approached you; but when I wake up from a flashback nightmare, it's that Robinson breaking ball that breaks me out in sweats.

The longer I write the more I remember about certain plate appearances. During Instruction League in the fall of 1977, a Yankees' right-hander named, Jim Colonel, threw me three sliders all in the same spot, low and outside, at the bottom of the knees, nipping the top right corner of the pentagon. I did not take the bat off of my shoulder. This inaction elicited a response from our third base coach Wayne Terwilliger, "You've got to swing the bat up there!" I wasn't in a position for a rebuttal, so I had to take Twig's loud dressing down, but in reality, at any level of baseball, from Little League to the Majors, I was not going to foul off any of those nasty sliders.

I can remember only one other pitch that captivated me similar to Colonel's sliders, and that was an 0-2 or 1-2 curveball from John Curtis in Anaheim. It wasn't in a big spot in the game or the season, but the pitch broke from an apex so high, and with a sharp, forceful loss of gravity, that decades later, I'm still wondering how I was supposed to attack that pitch.

Remember the last pitch of the 2006 National League Championship Series, the 0-2 curveball from Adam Wainwright to Carlos Beltran that sent the Cardinals to the World Series? You cannot hit that pitch, especially from a 6 ft. 7 in. right-hander with a mid-nineties fastball to complement the bowel-locking curve. I have heard people say that Beltran should have tried to at least foul the pitch off due to the magnitude of the game; oh, the temerity. Beltran is one of the best post-season performers ever. He's a .322 hitter with 16 homers, 45 runs scored and 40 RBIs in 56 games of the post-season. The importance of the game does not influence reaction time, the movement of the pitch determines reaction time.

I'll accept that my theory can be challenged. After all, I did not make a single post-season appearance, well, not in the majors anyway, though I did strikeout on three consecutive nasty curveballs during a media game from Travis, my youngest son's, godfather, Glenn Mekles, somewhere in Central Park in New York City. Down 0-2 in the count, it dawned on me that if Mekles strikes me out, I'd never hear the end of it, from one who sells medical insurance to hospitals. He has never bragged or even mentioned it to me, though that does not exclude a thousand other people who may know.

While I'm on memory lane, I got two pieces of advice that year that stuck with me. One was from third baseman

Don Thomas, who was a bit miffed after being sent down from Triple-A, "Always look after yourself, you can't be too nice!" He and his wife Brenda, were the most educated couple on the team, so it was easy to absorb his directive. The second piece of advice came from utility player, Mark Miller, who counseled me after I got the ass about being fined for some infraction that I'm sure I earned, but didn't want to pay. Heck, twenty-five dollars is a large percentage when you're netting less than six hundred dollars a month. He told me that I was going to the majors, so why let an incident in the minors be a bother? Ha, and I was the psychology major. Evidently not a very good one.

Triple-A ball was in Tucson, Arizona, home games at Hi Corbett Field, where General Manager, Jack Donovan had given us nicknames, and those names accompanied our real names as we were called out to our defensive positions at the start of the contests. For instance, our shortstop was Nelson 'Spiderman' Norman, a very apt description for a tall, thin, long-armed and legged, one-hand fielder from San Pedro de Macoris, the unofficial birthplace of major league shortstops. My nickname was 'The Wrist' which referred to my 'wait and be quick' swing. Long time major league pitching coach, Dick Pole, who I faced that season, still remembered my nickname years later in the majors, which was flattering to me. I did lead the league with 141 runs, playing in a team high 131 games in a 140 game season, so I'll happily accept all compliments.

Oh, and may I add, that we had only two scheduled off-days in the entire season. Arizona summers can be warm, as in three digits warm. One day on a 105 degree Phoenix afternoon, I left the hotel room to go across the street to eat a late lunch at a small restaurant, took six steps out of room, and turned right back to the air conditioned room. I deemed that I would lose more energy walking one-tenth of a mile than I would consume in nutrition and calories.

Due to the lighter air in the Pacific Coast League, which allowed the ball to travel further, the dimensions were deep, thus, allowing the cheap hits to fall safely. Double-digit scores were not unusual, especially in the southern division cities of Tucson, Phoenix and Albuquerque. The Tucson Toros had a .308 team batting average, yet, did not play .500 ball. I finished with a .352 average, which did not lead the league. In fact, it was only good for third.

Dodgers prospect Jeffrey Leonard, before he was two-flaps down in his home run trot, led the league in hitting, aided in some small part by an Albuquerque hometown scoring decision that didn't involve the Dodgers slugger. Well, not directly, though it involved me.

Going into the last week in the season, I trailed Leonard by four points and in my first plate appearance, I grounded a ball into the hole at short and the shortstop failed to field it cleanly on his backhand. The scoreboard flashed the 'H' sign for a hit, but by the time I had returned to first from my sprint across the bag, the scoreboard flashed the 'E' sign for error. I was livid. I knew what was going on. Had it been anyone else on our team, the hit would have stayed. But since I was so close to their star's batting average, I was not going to get closer to him on a marginal call, and finished the series seven points behind him amid an angst that lasted even after manager, Rich Donnelly, told me that I was going up to the big club after the end of our season. My 'thank you' response to Rich's announcement was a matter of fact one. I had given myself three or four years of minor league ball to make it to the majors and I was there on schedule.

The oldest looking 23 year old in all of Arizona in 1978

We finished the season just shy of a playoff spot, but here is a spoiler alert that I didn't realize until years later and something I addressed in my irreverent baseball clubhouse movie, *Reunion 108*; it is better for a player going to the majors to not make the Triple-A playoffs, both financially and for big league service time. I was making the massive sum of $1150 per month for the five months of Triple-A ball. The sixth month in the majors is prorated at the major league minimum, which was $21,000. Yes, I said $21,000 gross for the year in the double-digit inflation days of the late 1970s, not the over $507,500 minimum salary it is as I type today. The last month in the majors my check was $3500, which represented a $2350 increase, or more than double what I was making in the minors.

I know, if you are under forty years of age, it is difficult for you to even fathom professional athletic salaries so low, and to be honest with you, if I hadn't lived it, I'd probably have trouble absorbing that information as well. If it'll make it easier to understand, according to the Consumer Price Index of the Bureau of Labor Statistics, $21,000 dollars in 1979 computes to $73,368, and a dime, nickel and two pennies in 2016. I was born too early. I still think the latter salary number sounds better.

Pat Putnam and Nelson Norman were returning to the majors, while infielder, LaRue Washington; catcher, Greg Mahlberg; pitcher, Danny Darwin and I were going up for the first time. We were to meet the big club in Milwaukee. The Rangers were contending and were five and a half games out of first place. We started the early morning flights from Tucson to Phoenix, then Phoenix to Chicago. The afternoon leg was Chicago to Milwaukee and I have to admit, I was a little spent by the time I walked into the old visitor's clubhouse at County Stadium to see my name in the starting lineup, leading off.

Okay, I hadn't thought I'd play right away, but I'm okay with it. Well, assuming this is not a fake lineup of some sort. Dock Ellis walked by and said, "Good luck young man!" After a few moments, no one said anything to the contrary about the starting lineup, so I assumed it was the correct lineup for the evening and reality now started to sink in. I started to worry a bit, not because I was in the lineup, or even that I was leading off, but beside my last name was the position number 4 ... second base.

You remember from a few pages ago, just how adept I was as a second sacker in Double-A Tulsa? Well, I didn't even possess an infielder's glove, and my last glove should have been exorcised in some kind of outdoor barbecue ritual anyway. I turned to sportswriter, Paul Hagen and queried, "Doesn't Mr. Hunter know that I haven't played second base in over a year and a half?"

As we got there late in the afternoon, I didn't have time to seek an answer. It was time to stretch and run some sprints and get ready to earn a living at the major league level. In an attempt not to heighten the magnitude of the event, outfielder, Richie Zisk told me that, "This is just like Triple-A." I appreciated what he was trying to do, I didn't lack confidence, but it was a nice avuncular move nevertheless.

With about seven minutes before game time, manager Billy Hunter did call me over to explain my status for the evening. The coaching staff had felt that switch-hitting, second baseman Bump Wills was struggling a bit from his right side, so this was to give him a short mental, physical or psychological break I guess, and no matter how I fared at the plate, Bump was going to go into the game at second base. Well, that was a slight sigh of relief, before stepping into the batter's box and becoming the 11,691st player in major league history.

Left-hander, Jerry Augustine's first pitch, a low and outside sinking fastball was lined into right-center field.

Right-fielder, Sixto Lezcano, dove and it went off his glove for a base-hit. I'm standing on first base with a grin that could have been painted on, and here comes Bump to pinch-run for me, and even before he steals second, my day is over. My highest lifetime batting average is against the Brewers. Coincidence? I think not.

The Rangers did not close the gap toward first place and the defending division winning Kansas City Royals repeated in 1978. I get a few pinch-hits along the way and as I'm getting on the bus, after a 2 for 5 start with a double and a run scored in a 4-1 victory in our next-to-last game of the season in Seattle, the manager pats the seat to his left for me to join him. Billy Hunter starts to go over next year's team, going through the defensive positioning; Jim Sundberg will be behind the plate and Johnny Grubb and I are to platoon in left field.

This was sweet music to my ears. I was pleased to have made an impression on the manager in a relatively short amount of time. It really buoyed my spirits and my ego, which didn't get inflated often for any of us back in the day. A Tucson booster had told me that my great season in Triple-A was not a guarantee that I would stick in the majors. After all, prospects Pat Putnam, Gary Gray and Keith Smith had great Triple-A seasons, but still returned to the minors. I thought to myself, 'Tucson is a great city, a great place to play Triple-A ball, and I've had many good experiences, but I'm not coming back here other than to pick up my car.' Now I have confirmation from the head honcho himself ... The next day, the Rangers fired Billy Hunter.

Playing in the post-season was at the top of my to-do list for my major league career. That goal was not realized in my eight years and one month in the majors, so I don't have any climatic build-up to this narrative. In Texas we contended about every other year. In 1979 we finished the season with a 83-79 record, which was good enough for third place in a weak American League West. The California Angels took the division that year, their first post-season appearance since entering the league in 1961.

Their chant that year was "Yes, we can ... yes we can!" I was chasing a foul fly ball down the right-field line in Anaheim and I could feel the ground under me move with the force of the chanting and stomping in unison of the capacity crowd. I can only remember one other time when a collective sound was so loud, and that was in Milwaukee when Rangers' right-hander, Dave Schmidt, with the bases loaded and the game on the line, threw Robin Yount a 3-2 palm right down the heart of the plate for ball four. Such is life.

In the strike shortened 1981 season with split winners, we finished with an overall record of 57-48, a second place finish in the first half of the season and a third place finish in the second half. No one was sure at the time of the strike if there would be a settlement about free agent compensation, much less how the post-season participants would be selected. But because of a quirk of mathematics if we had won our last game before the strike, we would have been percentage points ahead of Oakland, though they would have been a half game ahead. The percentage points trumps the half-game lead. What makes this discovery even more nightmarish decades later is that we had a good chance to win the game in Milwaukee.

I had driven Buddy Bell and Mickey Rivers to the plate with a two-out single to center in the fourth inning, but with the score tied at three in the seventh, Buddy led off the inning with a triple off of Pete Vukovich. We had three chances to drive in the run with the infield in, and I was the second batter. After first baseman Pat Putnam popped to short, I was ahead of the count 3 balls, 1 strike. Rumor had it that the sinker-balling veteran right-hander had another pitch that went down in a hurry, more akin to the pitch disappearing into a trap door.

Now, I understand that both pitchers and hitters have pitches we'd like to have back. I don't have many, but of those I had, this is the one that agonizes me. I'm a contact hitter, he pitches to contact. If he has a 'swing and miss' pitch, this is the time to release it. At least that's what I'm thinking in the few seconds I can form cognitive thoughts between pitches. I waited for a fraction of a second longer in anticipation the sinker would become a super sinker; surprise, it was not the super sinker but the regular sinker. And instead of hitting it in the hole between third baseman, Don Money and shortstop, Robin Yount, I hit the ball hard, but right at Yount on the ground. I've concluded that with my luck, if I had been looking for the regular sinker, I would have gotten the super sinker, damned either way. Oh, and we don't score. In the bottom of the inning, Roy Howell hits a ball to parts unknown in Wisconsin for the game-winning blast.

In 1981, I also had one of the oddest 19 game hitting streaks in the history of baseball; it lasted 115 days. From April 18th-30th, I hit in eleven straight games, but in the seventh inning of the eleventh game, the Royals' U.L. Washington hit a line drive that stayed in the lights and by the time it cleared those low light stanchions in Arlington Stadium, I had very little room from the lowest tier of lights to the ground. In order to secure the catch, I rolled on my wrist, breaking the ulna styloid bone. I was on the disabled list before I knew it was officially broken. I was in the on-deck circle prior to going to the plate in the bottom of the inning, when it dawned on me that I couldn't swing (I usually took at least five swings before each plate appearance, the only minor superstition I had.) I caught a break however, when Royals' right-hander, Jim Wright hit me on the shoulder with a fastball.

I spent the entire month of May on the D.L. Clutch hitting Rick Lisi was called up for his only major league stint, and left the month with a 333 average. I rejoined the team after a three game minor league rehab stint, in which, ironically, I was hit on the same wrist I was rehabbing.

At that point I thought there was a chance I would never get out of the minor leagues. I placed a call to Don Zimmer and told him that I was ready. I had to get out of Oklahoma City before the minor league Grim Reaper claimed me. I met the team in Minnesota and hit in the next seven games to make it 18 straight, matching my career longest hitting streak of a year before, leading up to the biggest in-season labor impasse in major league history.

BILLY SAMPLE

IMPRESSIVE UNEMPLOYMENT

During the fifty-day strike over free agent compensation, the owners wanted to make the compensation for free agents as great if not greater than the value of the departing player, thus eliminating the 'free' part of free agency. The owners had also purchased strike insurance and it was so coincidental how the negotiations became serious as the length of the strike insurance declined.

For much of the impasse I was a disc jockey at KAAM in Dallas. Through Sports Director, Bret Lewis, I had a nightly, post-game Rangers report, which paid me eight thousand dollars for the season. Before I was arbitration eligible, the Rangers renewed my contract for the first two seasons, which may have been a baseball first. I had to have our Player Representative, Jon Matlack read the contract to me because I refused to sign it. When I became arbitration eligible, the club found its financial love for me and my gross for the year was one hundred thousand dollars. Remember that is gross; net may have been closer to seventy thousand.

Moonlighting in an industry that I was interested in was a good gig; the monetary compensation was much appreciated. Since KAAM radio was contractually obligated to pay me for the length of the baseball season anyway, they were going to get their money's worth. After sitting in with me for three hours playing middle of the road music, Bret left the studio, with me yelling, "Hey, wait, what are you doing?" I didn't have time to ask him what do I do if I need to use the bathroom. Richard Harris', MacArthur's Park was over seven minutes and on at least one occasion, that was not long enough. I wonder if anyone remembers that dead air aside from the station manager?

The owners pulled their final settlement offer a week before the eventual settlement, when some rumblings from uninformed players reached the press. Executive Director, Marvin Miller informed the ones who needed to be brought into the fold. A week later, the owners returned with exactly the same offer and a settlement was reached. Matlack not only had the often thankless job of dealing with union issues, but he was also the point person for any fan's ire during the labor impasse. Jon resigned his position to Rick Honeycutt, who also was on the pension committee of the union. I sat in on one of those meetings once and I would have understood what they were saying, except I missed a couple of classes of Mandarin Chinese along the way. That committee needed someone with a high aptitude test score, which I was sorely lacking. In 1982, Rick walked all of the union material across the clubhouse to my individual stall. And though I don't exactly remember volunteering for the role, Rick knew I had interest in labor affairs.

By the time I got the hang of the board, it was time to go back to work. My last song played, "While You See a Chance" by Steve Winwood. Associated Press photo

The 1981 season resumed with the All-Star game in August. Even with a .322 average, I had no chance of making the team, probably didn't even if I hadn't missed a month with the broken wrist. It's much easier for a borderline All-Star to make it today, with the expanded rosters. But not only did I never make an All-Star team, I never even made the All-Star game ballot. Only two outfielders per season made the ballot from Texas during the years I was there and I would never complain about any combination of Al Oliver, Richie Zisk, Mickey Rivers, George Wright, Larry Parrish or Gary Ward. But it would have been nice to have been nominated just once.

I was fortunate enough that even on teams that never made the playoffs, I was often privy to All-Star performances. During a double header in Detroit in 1980, Al Oliver went 6 for 9 that included four homers, a double and a triple. At some point I felt a bit guilty as I didn't have to pay to see that performance.

In 1981 utility player Bill Stein, nicknamed by me, 'The Trigger Man' for his ability to react to a high velocity first-pitch fastball, had an eighteen game hitting streak. Okay, that in itself is impressive, but not necessarily remarkable until you consider that seven of those eighteen hits were pinch-hits. The call would go up the runway for the veteran right-handed hitter, who would take his last gulp of coffee, toss aside the Styrofoam cup, stop by the on-deck circle for just a touch of pine tar, then proceed to hit a line drive somewhere. It seemed to always be a line drive, as his bat had a hair trigger during the stretch of games from May 2nd-31st.

Other impressive feats, in 1986: Dale Murphy had his consecutive games streak threatened when he jammed his hand through the Plexiglas in centerfield in Atlanta Fulton

County stadium. Not scheduled to play in the subsequent game against Doc Gooden and the Mets, Murphy pinch-hit, with stitches in his hand, and launched a curveball into the seats down the left field line. I had teammates who would have gone on the Disabled List with stitches in their hand ... seriously!

Later in that same year on July 6th, Bob Horner hit four homers in a game against the Montreal Expos, putting the former Arizona State star who spent no days in the minor leagues, in rarified company, becoming the eleventh player in major league history to accomplish the feat. Our kangaroo court fined the slugger, because he also became the second player who completed the feat in a game his team did not win. Obviously if he hits four homers in a game and we don't win, then he can't carry the club and what use is he?

Yes, even on a team, with middle of the road personalities, the kangaroo court system of fines can be brutal. One of the heaviest fines of my career occurred with the Braves. I was sitting on the bench during a game talking to a couple of players that included Chris Chambliss, the Yankees' 1976 Championship Series hero, now in a part-time role with the Braves. I wondered out loud why my former Texas Rangers manager, Doug Radar, wasn't fond of me, as if he was the only manager who wasn't. "I played hard, uniform always dirty, hustled after every ball, ran into fences with little or no fear ... I was a black guy who played white!" Chris brought me up on charges of uttering a racial slur, though I never could figure out which race I was slurring.

Wait, I'm not finished with impressive acts by teammates. I played outfield behind third baseman Buddy Bell, one of the best all around players in the game, for all six of his consecutive Gold Glove years. He played off the foul line, I covered ground to my right well into foul territory when needed for those rare occasions something got by him. We were a good defensive combination.

In 1985, I had a great view of Don Mattingly's Most Valuable Player season; anecdote forthcoming in a later chapter. I'm surprised that he only batted .324, because it didn't seem as though he made outs more than two-thirds of the time. He led the league in RBI (145), doubles (48), total bases (370), and sacrifice flies (15) adding to 35 homers, 107 runs scored and the first of his nine Gold Gloves. And if that wasn't enough, he struck out only 41 times in 727 plate appearances. No, I can't think of a present day player comparable to him either. Donnie Baseball never walked more than 61 times in his career. True, batting in front of Dave Winfield is not going to help your walk total, as pitchers have to challenge you more so as not to give free passes and potentially more RBIs to the batter behind you, but I credited his low walk total to Donnie's selflessness. If the situation called for the hitter to go out of the strike zone to help his team win, Mr. Mattingly was only too pleased to do so; sure, it cost him points on his batting average, and didn't help his numbers for the Hall of Fame, for which he has never gotten higher than 28.2 percent of the vote, but it endeared him forever to his peers who appreciate the way he played the game to win.

My final highlighted player of impressive acts is one John Milton "Mickey" Rivers, and his mold has never been recast. On one of those 100 degree Arlington afternoons, Mickey was speaking to a group of young kids in the stands. At some point he was instructing them on the rules of outfield play. "You have your long ball hitters and you have your short ball hitters, but more importantly, you have to check the wind-chill factor!" Now, there are about ten different responses one can have to that outfield playing ideology, and I chose the one that said Mickey simply misspoke, it happens to the best of us. But as the nighttime contest continued, I found myself wondering aloud if indeed the wind-chill had some bearing on the flight of the ball, and maybe Mickey was onto something that could be verified by scientists. Next time I see him, I'll ask if Miami Dade North offered classes in outfield meteorology.

One of my favorite 'Mick the Quick' stories occurred when infielder, Jeff Kunkel fouled a ball off the plate onto his face and could not continue at bat on August 9th, 1984 against the Red Sox. In the second inning of a scoreless contest there were runners at first and second, one out, and the call went out for our best pinch-hitter. The problem was that our best pinch-hitter hadn't anticipated coming into the game without the contest being in question and certainly not in the second inning. To give you a sense of where Mickey could have been, Jerry Jones' football stadium was decades from being built on the same grounds and that's an expensive cab ride from one end of the stadium to the other. There is no telling where Mickey could have been, he was a good hour and a half from needing to get ready on most nights. Since I was in the dugout, I have no idea how radio broadcasters, Mark Holtz and Eric Nadel filled the airtime in anticipation of whoever was the pinch-hitter to be.

Television mini-series have been shorter than the length of time it took Mickey to emerge from the runway to the dugout; his uniform top didn't match his pants, but it was close enough. His T-shirt didn't quite match the team colors, but that's just being picky and if he wanted to keep his running shoes on instead of changing into his spikes, well, that's his call. Without a warm-up swing, he fouls Al Nipper's first pitch back into the protective screen. The second pitch he rifles up the middle for an RBI single and a 1-0 lead in a game that we'd come from behind and win 7-3. For most of us, the game is simply not that easy.

One night when we all knew where Mickey was, had eye-opening results for me. He was in centerfield at Yankee Stadium, I was in left. Back in our day, the left-centerfield dimensions were 411 feet, not the 399 of today, then again, it wasn't the 457 of yesteryear. Point is, there is a lot of ground to cover, and on this evening we are conceding left-centerfield. If anyone is strong enough to carry a line drive over our heads, that person has earned it, and we'll try to hold him to a double. Sure enough, tonight's starting pitcher facing whoever the left-handed hitter was, pitched opposite of how we were positioned, though it didn't really matter, because the unremembered player hit a blast to left-center. I got a good jump on it, though I wasn't sure if I could catch it since it would have taken a "This Week in Baseball" dive and some luck to secure the ball after my bounced landing. Well, about a step before I was to leave my feet, Mickey glides to the ball in front of me for the putout.

As we crossed back to our positions, I must have had the most incredulous look on my face, because without speaking to him, Mickey volunteered, "Ah homey, I had him shaded that way!" Er, no, homey didn't have him shaded that way, I'm looking at him between each pitch so we wouldn't drift further apart than we had planned. No, Miami, Florida homey was swung around well into right-center. As I write this now, I still cannot comprehend how a human being could cover that much ground in such a short amount of time, and I wasn't exactly a tortoise my own self. Maybe, Mickey is not human. Does he have a bit of an alien look to you?

Without much doubt Mickey would be in the top whatever category of characters of the game of baseball. I had the opportunity to run into one of the characters of another sport in 1982. We were staying at the Edgewater Hyatt House across the street from the Oakland Alameda County Coliseum for a series with the Athletics, late enough in the summer for the Oakland Raiders to have their pre-season workouts. The hotel was constructed in a series of long mazes and one night after the game, I was trying to orchestrate my way to the hotel bar, er, ahem, hotel lobby. Amazingly my alcohol GPS was a little off and I entered a long corridor that took me away from my desired destination. About a third of the way down the hallway, a rather large man was attempting to open his hotel room door. He fumbled with his key and fell into a seated position. As he completed his fall, a large caliber gun dropped to his left toward me.

Thinking this is probably not exactly where I wanted to be, I began to pivot and turn toward the entrance from which I had arrived. Before I completed my turn, the man righted himself, spun to me and pointed the gun head high. As I anticipated the shot, I tried to put my body up against the hall space of a closed door to the room, wondering if I had left my widow enough life insurance. The bullet didn't come from the .357 Magnum, but the large gun-toter was moving toward me, with the gun still pointed head high. "Oh great, now he's going to pistol whip me!"

"What are you stealing?" Apparently, my jamming up against the hotel room door gave the appearance that I was stealing from a room I was leaving, as opposed to unsatisfactory shelter to prevent being killed. Now, I'm not a particularly voluble person, which is ironic since most of my post-baseball career has been as a broadcaster, but I became downright loquacious at this point. The big guy motions with the gun for me to walk down the hallway from the point that I was attempting to travel before he fell. I took two steps in that direction and then determined that I would die of a heart attack waiting to feel a blast in the back, so I walked back toward him, never staying further than arm's length or gun's length away.

This is where I became talkative and somehow persuaded the at least six-foot six or so guy, who appeared to be less unstable than mere moments ago, to walk down the hallway with me. I'm guessing he was on a mixture of alcohol and chemicals that I hadn't heard of and that's only speculation, because my main focus was staying within arm's length of the gun, thinking that he would not shoot me at point blank range and also he would have to concentrate more as we walked. Well, at the end of this long journey which probably only lasted ninety seconds but seemed like a lifetime, I recognized the guy, "Hey, you're John Matuszak aren't you?"

"Yeah, right-on!" And he opened the door and let me out into the parking lot. A police car had just passed us, but I was so glad the officer didn't see him, me or the gun, because that had the making of someone really getting hurt. By the way Matuszak was six-foot eight.

There is a short addendum to the John Matuszak anecdote. He was doing the promotional tour for his book, *Cruisin' with the Tooz*, and had an interview scheduled with Richard Neer of WNEW in New York City, where I was also working as a reporter. After the interview, just before he left, I told him, "I have my own John Matuszak story. I was walking down a long hallway in a hotel in Oakland when a guy falls trying to open his hotel room door."

"The night with the gun," he interrupts. He gives me a big hug full of apologies, turns the corner, backtracks quickly, raises his hands in the shape of a gun and says, "Stick 'em up!"

Ha-ha-ha ... grrr ... with a moderate forced grin. Over the years since our initial interaction, I have run into a number of people who have great things to say about John, some have acknowledged the wilder side, but all in all he would be the kind of guy I'd like to hang with. We have so much in common, being athletes, actors and such, he was in *North Dallas Forty* and the *Goonies* among other movies and ... I get to live to tell about it, which something Tooz unfortunately didn't get much more of a chance to do. Two years later, John's heart gave out; hard living had caught up to him. He was only 38.

HAPPY TRAILS ... START SPREADING THE NEWS

It was time to go, I had worn out my welcome in Arlington, never could quite get over the hump. In spite of a weak second half, 1983 was somewhat of a breakout season. If I put together an even better season the following year maybe I can make a career out of this. But it didn't happen; 1984 was the worst season of my career. I had a horrendous season, finishing with a .247 average. The season started poorly and finished worse.

Oh, there were some mitigating circumstances, but it's not as if I can put an asterisk beside the putrid numbers. My wife, Debi, had her first diagnosed multiple sclerosis attack and spent two months at Johns Hopkins hospital in Baltimore. I was trying to raise two young children, Nikki and Ian, with the help of our babysitter, Sharon Finnegan of Euless and the help of friends like Pat and Tommy Talbott of Ft. Worth, while flying up to Baltimore on off days.

On the field, the Rangers had traded for outfielder Gary Ward, who had gotten off to a slow start playing right-field, so he was shifted back to left, his position in Minnesota where he had the most success, and in the draft, the Rangers had selected Oddibe McDowell with their first pick, and the Olympian was in the majors for good by 1985.

I tried to ease my exit as best I could, quietly, yet with firm statements. Local sports anchor and friend, Paul Crane hosted a segment in the off-season that allowed me to say goodbye, affirming that there were no hard feelings, it was just time. I usually went to spring training at least ten days before the reporting date; however, in the spring of 1985, I arrived closer to the deadline. The Rangers' camp in Pompano Beach, Florida, opened a day before the other local camps, and after our first workout, I got the word that I had been traded to the New York Yankees. The best part about that, other than going to a contending club, was that I didn't have to move, since the Yankees trained in Ft. Lauderdale, not even fifteen minutes away.

Fifteen minutes in travel time, but light years apart in accommodations. I really enjoyed Pompano Beach, after all, the city has a Sample Road. How can one not like the place? But the spring training facility was like something out of a bad dream. There were two fields, neither of which were decent. To show you how bad they were, the back field was referred to as Iwo Jima. The front field, where the games were played, had such uneven turf and dirt that bad hops resulted in a broken nose for shortstop Mark Wagner and a broken jaw for second baseman Mike Richardt. The outfield had crab grass so thick that it seemed to grab your ankles with your first crossover step. There was a blimp that was housed in the sight-line of the left-fielder; and believe me, you haven't lived until you've had Dale Murphy drop a clothesline hanging line drive at you coming out of a large silver object in the background.

There were times when we didn't have even one working pitching machine. Now, not every player likes hitting off the machines as it can disrupt timing with an inconsistent dropping of the ball into the chute; however, early in spring training a number of us hitters would like to build hand and forearm strength. Having to rely on batting practice pitchers or coaches for BP, with such small real estate, doesn't even guarantee a hitter would get thirty swings per day, and the fans have a right to know why their team is at the bottom of the offensive categories. By contrast, the Yankees had six cages of pitching machines, and each machine was set to a different pitch and velocity. We hit so much, I was tired of hitting. My blisters had blisters.

On the main field where batting practice was held and available to the public, fans would cheer when a nice catch was made. I liked getting in my defensive work off of live BP, and I was starting to feel like I was mugging for the audience as they applauded so much. When I reached the facility in Ft. Lauderdale, I had an impromptu press conference, and someone must have told owner George Steinbrenner that I sounded good, because he came to my clubhouse stall and welcomed me to the club. I appreciated that gesture; it wasn't like welcoming Rickey Henderson to the team, I was at best a fourth or fifth outfielder on a team with Henderson, Dave Winfield and Ken Griffey Sr.

Growing up in the mountains of southwest Virginia during the 1960s, the only televised baseball I saw was the *Game of The Week*, and even during the losing years of the mid-sixties to mid-seventies, because of the media market, the Yankees were often on the tube. I could mimic Bobby Richardson's batting stance and I knew that on those rare occasions that Tony Kubek struck out, he sprinted back to the dugout as if he was embarrassed to be on the field of play. It has been a bit of a thrill for me, and I am not prone to being awed, to interact with players I watched while growing up. Warning, do not speak at an event behind Bobby, he's an evangelical minister who can speak for fifty-five minutes without a pause and don't ever try to beat Tony to the ballpark as a broadcaster; I've tried, can't be done. Once I was ready to congratulate myself, I had in fact nearly raised my hands in triumph only to see him there reading the newspaper at 2:30 for a 7:35 game time start. At charity events in the New York area, Joe Pepitone will kid me as if we were teammates, and I was seven years old when he made it to the majors.

All of this to say that I had some Yankees beginnings, however, I had been playing against the Yankees for over six years, and the trade didn't have me embracing all of the pinstripe mystique overnight. Also, James Cagney was not singing Yankee Doodle Dandy in my head. While with the Rangers, I once had an umpire indicate to me that he wasn't going to have catcher, Rick Cerone, show him up in front of a sold-out crowd at Yankees stadium. The connotative meaning was that a close pitch, even if it was off the plate, would most likely go in the Yankees' favor. Now, nothing against Rick, he had a very nice seventeen year career, and I have a lot of fun hanging with him when circumstances permits, but he's not Bill Dickey or Yogi Berra or Thurman Munson. Why does my strike zone have to be wider?

Well, I guess it was good that I didn't bathe in the glow of being a Yankee as I was only there for the 1985 season, but what a season it was. No, we didn't make the playoffs. We would have had to sweep the Blue Jays in the season's last series in Toronto, and then win a make-up game. Winning the first game was a tease, but former disgruntled Yankee, Doyle Alexander, was pitching game two, and he exacted his revenge. In our last game of the year, Phil Niekro notched his 300th career victory. He threw only one knuckleball, which disposed of Jeff Burroughs for the game's final out, a strikeout. During the off-season, while at our union meetings in Maui, General Manager Clyde King called to tell me I had been traded to Atlanta for a minor league infielder, Miguel Sosa. Well, it wasn't a shock, but I didn't really beg out as I had the previous year in Texas.

I have mentioned from time to time that I have Daffy Duck legs; big thighs, big feet, small ankles and cattle-rustler stolen calves, and it's the lack of calves that makes the use of stirrups confounding. I complained about the stirrups in a July 6, 1987 Sports Illustrated article. To keep them up, I tried adhesive tape, rubber bands, Velcro, electrical tape; nothing seemed to keep the stirrups up on my skinny calves without cutting off circulation. After a year in the big leagues, I discovered a company that made stirrups with very little material that allowed me to hook them onto my sliding kneepads and they stayed up without falling, just like those of my grown-up teammates. Through some stroke of serendipity, I had bought several pairs of those stirrups that matched the midnight bluish colors of the Yankees when I was buying the color that matched the brighter blue of the Rangers. Clubhouse manager, Nick Priore, saw the stirrups and told me that I couldn't wear those with the Yankees. Oh dear, what's a brother to do? He finds two other brothers, who have a lot of clout; Rickey Henderson and Dave Winfield, who liked them a lot. The next day we all had them on, and I didn't hear another word about them. And that, boys and girls is how the Yankees began wearing the stirrups of this generation.

The stirrups of the Daffy Duck Generation

Also, those very comfortable Brooks mesh shoes. They were excellent, unless it rained

Rickey had an ankle injury that postponed his start of the regular season, a season that started with a Red Sox sweep of the Yankees at Fenway. It appeared that the pressure was on Yogi from the start. I have to admit, I was not aware of the Yankees-Red Sox fierce rivalry. I'd see an occasional fight between the two clubs, but in Texas it seemed we were always fighting the Royals, Angels or A's, so I didn't realize the two eastern clubs took the rivalry so personally. And I only knew about the desire for a subway series between the Yankees and Mets (before inter-league play) when a media member rather callously asked me, "Wouldn't it be great to have a subway (World) Series?" Well, yes, it would be, except I was a member of the Texas Rangers at the time!

The Rangers played well against the Red Sox, and I had some good games against them too. I had played them often enough to know that when they have their hitting shoes on, as they did in the opening series against the Yankees, there isn't much you can do except take your whipping. In August, we returned the favor at Yankee Stadium with a four game sweep that virtually eliminated them from post-season contention. Randolph, Henderson and yours truly had great catches in that series capped off by a breathtaking catch by Ken Griffey off the bat of Marty Barrett. Ken went into the stands, brought the would-be homer back into the ballpark and executed a backflip on his way back into the field of play. Another exceptional feat by a teammate and a game saving play at that.

Back to the opening weeks of the season. The club rebounded somewhat and was 6-7 after salvaging the last game of the Red Sox series a week later in the Bronx. Boston had taken five of the first six meetings of the year, which put some heat on the club. The heat produced moderate speculation about the coaching staff's security. But as we flew into the Windy City for a three game series with the White Sox, the heat became a full-blown Chicago fire; you could cut the tension with a knife. Four of the eight managers I worked under were fired during the season, and once the speculation had lasted over a week, the unsettled atmosphere had a way of disrupting focus, making it harder for the team to perform.

With that as a backdrop, the team lost the three games in Chicago to fall to 6-10, and Yogi was relieved of his duties. Shortly after we got the news of Yogi's firing and Billy Martin's rehiring, a trash can flew across the room in what I imagine was an act of homage for our fallen manager. I can't swear to you who threw it, but if you said it was a six-foot two, two hundred twenty-five pound native of Austin, Texas, who stood right on top of the plate and got hit a lot, I wouldn't argue with you. Whoever it was, when news of this action got back to the new manager, it helped the employment of longtime power-hitting outfielder Willie Horton, as our new Tranquility Coach. In other words, Willie would make sure our trash can thrower (or anyone else), would not enter into a possible physical discussion with our smallish, but game, recycled manager.

On our way to O'Hare after the game, the bus stopped to let Yogi off before we got to our plane. I'm choked up more now writing about it than I was then. Everyone loved and respected Yogi. I was very flattered when he came to me in the batting practice outfield, to tell me he'd try to get me in the lineup whenever he could. Yet, no matter how iconic a personality, I had been conditioned to managerial firings. He didn't deserve it, especially the way it came down with the promise of a longer tenure, but it happened and will continue to happen.

I allowed myself to feel sentiment only once. It was at the end of my first minor league spring training when catcher-first basemen-outfielder, Alphonso Lewis was released. Drafted in the ninth round, a round ahead of me, we had played rookie ball together the previous year. He had performed as well as or better than a couple of the higher draft picks, but the higher picks had more money invested in them and when it came to a numbers game, Alphonso was released. I teared up when he talked about how he would be viewed as a failure when he returned to Pensacola, Florida. That was my last baseball related tear.

The new manager, Billy Martin met the team in Arlington, Texas, the place of his residence, well, for that matter, it was the place of my residence too. Billy and I crossed paths under the bleachers on the third base side of the outfield, and he said he'd try to get me in whenever he could. Hmm, sounds familiar. I think every manager says that. I told him I understood and I'd be ready for whenever that situation presented itself. I was in college when Billy managed the Rangers in the mid-seventies, but I had played against him when he managed Oakland and knew the type of game he managed. Billy Ball was aggressive; bunts and hit-and-runs as much if not more than the three-run homers. Well, it's easier to control the small ball than the three-run homer. I was not aware that Billy and I had any history. I remember only one fight with Oakland when I was with Texas, and it was when Danny Darwin hit Cliff Johnson hip-high. After the subsequent plate appearance and groundout, Johnson confronted Darwin on the mound and some hands were thrown all around, but I didn't throw any.

Well, it appears that maybe I did raise the ire of Mr. Martin in some capacity. After my playing days, I broadcasted with the Atlanta Braves, and before a game in San Diego in 1988, Rich 'Goose' Gossage, now with the Padres, called me over under the bleachers on the third base side of the field (I know, has every baseball conversation I've had been conducted under the bleachers?) Goose asked me how I got along with Billy. I said that I didn't think he was crazy about me, but I didn't dislike him. It appears that in Goose's first year with the Yankees, Martin told him to hit me in the head in spring training. Initially, I thought Goose had his timeline off, but he gave me a look as if he'd been internalizing that directive for longer than he'd care to remember. Actually, that incident has made three books: Roger Kahn's *October Men* (he also wrote *Boys of Summer*), Reggie Jackson's book, *The Life and Thunderous Career of Baseball's Mr. October*, and Goose's book, *The Goose is Loose*.

I thanked Goose for not carrying out orders, orders that could have been disastrous for me. I was fortunate to only get hit once in the head, and that pitcher threw nowhere near as hard as Goose's 98 mph fastball running into a right-handed hitter; add to it that corkscrew delivery that makes it a bit harder to pick up the pitch. I remember Goose hitting Ron Cey in the head in the 8th inning of Game 5 of the 1981 World Series and thinking that if that pitch had been an inch lower to Cey's temple, the Penguin would be a dead man. I often wonder if I'm being a little melodramatic about my potentially precarious position. It's not as though I haven't seen people get hit in the head by a pitched ball. One of the first times was from the on-deck circle of an American Legion game, when Al Holland hit Scott Atkins in the head with a mid-nineties fastball. Down went Atkins. We all went to him as he stayed down for twenty or so seconds, rose, shook his head free of cobwebs and went to first base. (And yes Al or Alfred as we knew him back then is the same guy who was the National League Fireman of the Year for the World Series bound Philadelphia Phillies in 1983). There was no concussion protocol back in the day. You either went to first, or went to the morgue, ha. I've run into Goose a few times since we first discussed that managerial demand ... it still ruffles him.

In spite of winning 97 games, the 1985 Yankees spent no days in first place, and that's with a team of Henderson, Winfield, Randolph and Mattingly. It's also with Ron Guidry having a bounce back season, with the best winning percentage in the league with a 22-6 record. Mike Pagliarulo aided in Gator's winning form by playing Gold Glove caliber third base, catching everything from right-hand hitters rolling over on Louisiana Lightning's off-speed pitches. Rookie, Brian Fisher, bridged our bullpen to closer Dave Righetti and his 28 saves, while picking up 14 saves of his own, with a three to one, strikeout to walk ratio and a 2.38 earned run average. And getting back to the offense, the Yankees led the league, well, led the majors with runs scored, averaging 5.21 per contest. We didn't lead the league in hits, but the hits weren't as important when Henderson leads off the game with a walk, steals second, Randolph hits the ball to the right side to move him to third and Mattingly hits a grounder to the infield playing at normal depth, easily scoring Henderson.

As impressive as the performances were in the Bronx, they were equally impressive in Toronto. The outfielders alone would carry them for some time to come; George Bell, Lloyd Moseby and Jesse Barfield were coming into their own and they averaged playing in 155 of the 162 games. The pitching staff was led by Dave Stieb, Jimmy Key and Jim Clancy, and if that was not enough, right-hander, Dennis Lamp was 11-0 coming out of the bullpen. Bill Caudill was their early season stopper to finish games, but the player who I thought was the difference in the two games between the Blue Jays and the Yankees didn't come up from the minors until July 29th. In his first ten outings, Tom Henke had three wins and seven saves.

Henke ... Henke, that names sounds familiar, oh wait, that was my former teammate in Texas. He couldn't quite put it together in Arlington, but found a career elsewhere. Henke, and two first round picks, Righetti and Ron Darling, as well as Walt Terrell and Len Barker, were all former Rangers pitchers who found careers elsewhere. Oh, and just for the record, Righetti was a 'throw in' in a ten player trade between the Rangers and Yankees in November of 1978, later becoming the American League Rookie of the Year in 1981. I'll have to switch subjects, I feel my blood pressure rising. Instead of having a dominant Righetti as a longtime teammate in Texas (and we played Instructional Ball together in 1977), I now get to face him, amassing only 4 non-productive singles in 17 at bats, while striking out 5 times. Thanks!

I'm guessing most of you have seen the play from August 2nd, where Carlton Fisk tags two runners out at the plate off of the same throw. Well, in all honesty, if you had taken a poll in the clubhouse before the game and presented the exact scenario and asked, "What two players would be involved in this strange play?" On eighty percent of the ballots, the answers would have been Bobby Meacham and Dale Berra; and it only *sounds* like I'm throwing them under the bus, because I understand how it happened. Understanding still didn't take away the 'You've got to be bleeping me' factor, with mouths agape. Wait, that's White Sox broadcaster Ken 'Hawk' Harrelson's line and he was there to watch this play too.

Andre Robertson leads off the bottom of the seventh of a game tied at three, with a single. Meacham pinch-runs. Do you remember the infamous Pine Tar Game when George Brett was ruled out after apparently hitting a go-ahead 2-run homer? Andre's promising career was hindered the same night after being involved in a car wreck on Manhattan's West Side Highway in which he broke the C-2 vertebrae in his neck. Back to this unforgettable play, Berra's ground ball to short was booted by Ozzie Guillen. Now, here is where the fun begins. Rickey Henderson hits a laser to left-centerfield, but closer to center. From his position halfway off second base, Bobby can't tell if center-fielder Luis Salazar can get to the drive, especially after the fielder throws up his glove as a decoy to catching the ball; Dale, from his lead at first can tell that Salazar is not going to flag it down, and knows he should score. Bobby, again, thinking that Salazar is going to catch the ball, goes back to second to tag up and advance to third, but as he pushes away from second, he slips, and Dale is only a few strides behind him.

Salazar efficiently gets the ball back to shortstop Guillen, in the cut-off position, who atones for his error earlier in the inning by making a strong one-hop throw to the plate. Third base coach, Stick Michael is having a nightmare in front of twenty-seven thousand people, as both runners are rounding third virtually at the same time. Fisk, after applying the tag to the lead runner, spins around from Meacham's inertia, to greet Berra's futile attempt to score standing up. The television director in my mind pans to Yankees dugout; fifteen players with mouths open in utter disbelief. White Sox win in twelve innings, 6-5.

An incredible amount of sex appeal in one photo. Both players scored at least 41 percent of the time they were on base. The speedster on the right, a major league record amount of times

Later in August, I had my Yankees' half-inning. I played in only 59 games and some of those appearances were very short. I remember once in Baltimore, I had an RBI single my first at bat, only to be removed for a pinch-hitter the second time up with a lead and the bases loaded in the second inning. Heck, was only so much complaining I could do, as Ken Griffey Sr. was the pinch-hitter, a .296 lifetime hitter with an All-Star Game MVP and a couple of

World Series rings. I remember Kenny trying to rush home to see the older of his two athletic sons, a two-sports star at Moeller High School in Cincinnati. The son, a left-handed hitter, never seemed to have good days on the ball field when his dad was around. Hmm, I wonder what happened to him?

Anyway, there was a late starting pitching change by the Red Sox that changed our lineup to more of a right-handed hitting version. In the seventh inning, we were protecting a one-run lead, as the Sox had the bases loaded (or drunk, if you prefer) with one out. Marty Barrett hits a line drive sinking in left-center field. I made the catch with a headfirst dive and came up throwing to second base, where my momentum had taken me. For some reason Jim Rice failed to tag and scored from third. It was a moot point because after Bob Shirley replaced Rich Bordi on the mound, Wade Boggs singled to left scoring Rice and my one-hop throw to catcher Butch Wynegar was ruled to be in time to retire Rich Gedman trying to score from second. Gedman jumped in the face of plate umpire Don Denkinger, complaining that Butch didn't tag him, but Gedman had a pop-up slide at the plate, which really didn't allow the umpire to see where the shoe stopped in relationship to the plate, especially with the dirt flying.

I was satisfied; not a bad half-inning defensively. Mattingly doubles in the game winning runs and I'm holding court with the media. Heck, they could get Donnie's comments about being the hero any of five days during the week. A media member asked if that was my biggest play of my career, relative to the magnitude of the event, and I went all the way back to high school football; my Andrew Lewis Wolverines versus the E.C. Glass Hilltoppers in the State Regionals and scoring the winning touchdown, the third of three by our Salem, Virginia based team in a minute forty-six seconds to erase a 14-0 domination. A win later, we advanced to the State Finals to play another undefeated team, T.C. Williams High School from Alexandria, Virginia, whose exploits were memorialized in the movie, *Remember the Titans.*

I won't say who won that game, but it would have been hard for them to make the movie had they lost. I was so impressed that renowned sportswriter, Phil Pepe could keep all of that straight in his column. A little bit of the air was taken out of my balloon of accomplishment that day however, as Wynegar admitted to the media that he really didn't tag Gedman, which didn't lend itself to making Denkinger look or feel good, so Butch sought him out the next day in the umpires' room to offer an apology.

Earlier in the book I mentioned that I have a Don Mattingly anecdote. I'm hesitant to tell it because it happened near the dugout and that and the clubhouse is the players' sanctuary, but I've told Donnie that I've mentioned it before, and it is rather innocuous in the scheme of things. The Evansville, Indiana native with the Popeye forearms is my only teammate who had an MVP season of the nine seasons I played. He was going so good in 1985 that he could take time to enjoy the moment, even if he didn't succeed in that said moment. In Game Three of a three game series hosting the Mariners, hard throwing 22-year-old Edwin Nunez broke off a nasty 1-2 curveball, that somehow Donnie got a piece of to foul it off at the plate. You could almost see the unspoken language between the two competitors, "Hey, if you hit my nastiest breaking pitch, I'm not going to waste throwing it again!"

And here comes a fastball ... it was fouled back, how about another fastball ... fouled back again. You know you're getting another fastball, you like 97 miles? Well, Nunez threw that fastball past the Yankees first baseman, the second time he fanned Mattingly in the series. Donnie walks back to the dugout, exclaiming, "I love it, he challenged me, I loved it!" Upon which, this Billy, the omniscient author and teammate throughout this exchange, is somewhere between puzzlement and extreme admiration for seeing someone so comfortably confident in their work, that the challenge, regardless of the outcome, is much appreciated.

Incoming! Outfielder stealing my foul fly-ball souvenir. I actually remembered to give the paying patron a replacement ball before taking my left-field position in the next inning

WHAT WE HAVE HERE
IS A FAILURE TO COMMUNICATE

One of the beauties of baseball and also an area of potential conflict is the differences in subjective analysis; what you think is fair and equitable on the playing field is probably not the same as I think. On July 11th, Rangers' 5 foot 11 right-hander, Glen Cook, making his fourth major league start, gives up a home run to Dave Winfield in the bottom of the first inning, and hits the next batter Ron Hassey. It didn't seem intentional to me, and I doubt it did to most of us, it looked like he hung onto a slider too long, but it did hit Hassey solidly. In the second inning, Willie Randolph takes Cook deep and after retiring the next batter, Cook hits Bobby Meacham. Again, it didn't appear to be intentional, sometimes people get hit. I should say though, that I was hit much more in one year of professional ball than I was hit in all of amateur years, going all the way back to Little League. Anyway, as with Hassey, Meacham was hit solidly.

Now, here is where subjectivity takes over. Even if you feel that Cook was innocent of purposeful plunking, do you offer a physical rebuttal? Would you wait until he hits a third person, knowing at that point even the Rangers might anticipate some return fire? Watching the game from the stands or the dugout or at home, we could come up with fifty different hypotheses for what could happen next. If I were managing, I might let the two hit by pitches slide, though if anyone came close to getting hit again, someone is going to get neck-tied, especially if we had the lead, then again, we don't all think alike. I think in most, but not all situations, if a retaliatory pitch is forthcoming, it's done on the first pitch, either a hit by pitch in the back or hip, or maybe a pitch well over the head or maybe around the chin, lips or forehead. I'm just sayin', that's my philosophy.

Our starter Joe Cowley threw Rangers shortstop Curtis Wilkerson, leading off the top of the third, a first pitch fastball strike, usually an indicator that nothing is up retaliatory speaking at this juncture of the contest. The second pitch, another fastball, hits the switch-hitting Wilkerson in the head. Tough program here, I thought it was a bit over the top, but evidently not everyone felt that way. 'Sweetness' as I nicknamed Curtis when were teammates because of his smoothness in the field, was felled and groggy, but managed to stay in the game until Wayne Tolleson replaced him in the field in the fifth inning. The only concussion tests back in the day was to have the trainer hold a select numbers of fingers in front of your face and ask you to identify the number(s). At this point, it's the Rangers move, if they felt our retaliation was over the top. I'm guessing a hit by pitch in the ribs, though intentional, may not have raised the ante, but a pitch bouncing off the helmet, might cause this hitting thing to escalate.

What transpired next falls into my category of 'Most Impressive Athletic Feats in Baseball'. After all of these years, it ranks number two and please don't ask me number one, because I can't tell you. The second batter in the inning, Oddibe McDowell singles to right; runners at first and second with no one out. The third batter of the inning, Toby Harrah, who was traded back to Texas in my deal to the Yankees, chopped a ball off of the plate towards first. Now, I had heard that Toby was one of the best athletes to come out of the state of West Virginia, and this confirmed it for me. How he could take a 90 mph fastball running in on his hands, hit it towards first, too far for the catcher to field, not far enough for the first baseman to field, and close enough to the foul line to have the pitcher field it. Then, make contact with the pitcher to run Cowley over, breaking his nose in the process; it is absolutely one of the most incredible feats I have seen in all of my years.

Now, watching it on replay, you could tell Toby took a step out of the baseline to shoulder and forearm Joe, but as it went down live, it looked like a legitimate play. Oh, Toby went through the ruse of calling his former Texas manager, Billy Martin to apologize for the unfortunate play of happenstance, but we all knew how the game is played, and that was in the era of the players policing the game themselves, well at least for that afternoon. Now, I don't know if Toby feels there is a statute of limitations on this play, but don't force him to lie by asking about it, though he may just give you a smile and a wink.

I have three other incidents of players policing the game from back in the day, though I have to admit, I appreciate how much more power ownership has given the umpires to limit the kinds of tit for tat players dealt with from my generation. I think there is a great correlation between offense and revenue and thus hitters are more protected nowadays. If the two batters in front of you hit homers and you were hit in the neck on the next pitch, even your teammates would have told you, "Dude, you should have been on your toes!" Today, the similar scenario could result in the pitcher being immediately ejected.

In 1978, twenty-eight year old Triple-A teammate, Stan Thomas, who had spent a few seasons in the majors, was trying to make his way back up to the big leagues. He was pitching one night at home in Tucson. Left-handed hitting Bobby Jones, who later became a teammate in Texas, hit a long grand slam against the right-handed pitcher. Thomas' first pitch to the next batter, Willie Aikens, hit the powerful left-handed hitter in the ribs. Your sweet and naive great-grandmother would have thought, 'yep, that was intentional.' The Salt Lake City Angels went on to blow the game open, and in the meantime, their manager, old school former major leaguer, Deron Johnson, was ejected from the game that inning arguing a call. After the rather obvious looking 'hit by pitch', I calculated who the first batter in the next half-inning would be ... hmm, wait, dang, it's me.

Because the game was no longer a contest and their manager had been ejected, I really thought I might have escaped a ... 'Bam!' Dominican right-hander, Carlos Julio Perez threw a mid-90s zone-changing fastball, which exploded into my hip. I hobble back to the backstop and was pissed, pissed enough to fight Perez even though I knew somewhere in the not too deep recesses of my brain, that I was really not on the moral high ground here. I limped past Thomas in the dugout who was conscious enough of the situation not to make eye contact, especially with a guy who just took a fastball ten to twelve miles per hour harder than he had delivered to Aikens.

A year later in the majors, I was put into another precarious situation. On a 101 degree day in Arlington, Angels pitchers, Jim Barr and Ralph Botting retired only three batters, and were charged with 12 runs, 11 of them earned. In the bottom of the third with Pat Putnam at first from a hit-by-pitch, and us trying to add to a 12-0 lead, Eric Soderholm, swung at a 3-0 pitch and flied to centerfield. I was in the on-deck circle applying the last touches of pine tar on my bat thinking, 'I must have missed a pitch (a strike) somewhere, because I know Soderholm didn't swing at a 3-0 pitch with a double-digit lead, no matter how early in the game it is.' As I walked to the plate from the first base side of the field, I was thinking that unless I can find that elusive strike call, I could be in a little trouble.

I hear Angels manager, Jim Fregosi, yelling to get their catcher, Brian Downing's attention. He does and points at his own head, but meaning mine. I intercept the gesture and give Fregosi an 'Aw come on' look, to which the former shortstop tells me, "Well, somebody has got to pay!" Well, I managed to strike out during the plate appearance, but was still pleased that I was aware enough of the situation to look into the Angels' dugout, as either of the first two pitches from right-hander Steve Eddy might have hit me in the chin. When the count went to 3-1, Fregosi got Downing's attention again. I should have bailed for a third time, but I didn't think they'd throw at me again. And yet, they did, this time hitting my bat, nearly knocking it out of my hands in my defensive position. The full count pitch was a stroke of genius, a middle of the plate fastball that I had planned to undress Eddy with a line drive up the middle. Well, until I began to swing and the pitch became a slider; checked swing strike-three. Well played Halos.

In the next half-inning, Fergie Jenkins threw the first pitch behind (Disco) Dan Ford's extremely closed batting stance, and we were all even for the afternoon. The game was really never in question, though the Angels did manage to score some runs to make the final 14-4. I went up to Soderholm after the game to ascertain if he and I were on the same page about that 3-0 swing. I only remember receiving somewhat of a blank stare from Eric that didn't confirm or deny the existence of my concerns. I did drive in four of the fourteen runs in the victory, I would have to be satisfied with that.

Later that summer I had another period of good timing, when I was batting behind Willie Montanez in the lineup. Willie's first and only stint in the American League began in August and to say that the native of Catano, Puerto Rico had a little showman in him, well, would be a slight understatement. Okay, a moderate understatement. Heck, why be coy, he was just some pickle relish shy of a hot dog.

As the ball carries very well in right-center field in the Ballpark in Arlington (Globe Life Park) nowadays, drives in the old ballpark just died in that direction. Your name had to be Singleton, Murray or Jackson to leave the yard on a blast to right-center. What was even more disheartening for a hitter was the ball would parachute and not sink, allowing the outfielders time to run down the would-be extra base hits. I can still picture Angels' first baseman, Ron Fairly, putting together a unique combination of curse words crossing the diamond after having his best blast ending up in the glove of the right fielder.

Anyway, Montanez turns on a Roger Erickson fastball and hits it low enough that the wind doesn't make a play on the ball and it clears the fence for a homer. I don't remember if he handed the batboy his bat before he got to first, but when he hit first base, he trotted deep into the infield skin towards where he hit the blast, he touched second base and then slow trotted towards left-centerfield. He stepped on third base and walked, yes, walked the last five steps to the plate. Up until this point, I had never heard Twins' catcher Butch Wynegar speak. His release from muteness was quite audible as he had walked halfway to the mound in incredulity, "I can't believe ... did you see what ... I can't believe they let him get away with ... are you kidding me?"

Now, I was seriously as amazed as Butch, but even if I wasn't, I was going to give it my best thespian, "Butch, I'm with you man, that was unbelievable, they let him do that in the National League? I'm sorry Butch, I'll need to have a word with him about that." Sure Billy, the guy has been in the majors for fourteen years, and you're going to have a word with him. It didn't matter, I was just trying to get on Butch's good side as quickly as possible. Erickson once threw behind Bobby Grich in Bloomington, Minnesota; it was on film. I was a bit strong for my size, but nowhere near as physically imposing as the 6 ft. 2 in. Grich. I was not digging in. I didn't get hit. Thank you Butch and Roger, I just didn't feel like getting hit that evening.

And it was not like I was afraid of getting hit. In 1981 I was fourth in the league in getting hit by the pitch and I missed a month of the season. In 2798 career plate appearances, I was hit 28 times. By extreme comparison, John Kruk was hit twice in 4603 plate appearances and Ken Griffey Sr., with 5,051 more plate appearances than me at 8,049, was hit only 14 times.

Okay, one more hit by pitch story and then I'll return to pinstripes. On another one of those hot August nights in

Arlington, Red Sox pitcher Bob Stanley hit me on the left knee with one of those hard sinkers, and at 6 ft. 5 in., that sinker covers a lot of area. As he released the pitch, he and his catcher, Gary Allenson, yelled, "Look out!" 'Aw, how nice,' I thought, as I limped to the dugout; only on rare occasions had anyone realized so early in the release of the cowhide to follow it with a warning.

Nice or not, since that evening, I've had problems with that knee, three of my five arthroscopes have been on that side. Heck, discomfort comes with the territory, and I'm sure I am not the only one who suffers from bouts of arthritis from physical exertion. One night, years after my last ground ball to short, as I was going through my career, I shot up from a deep sleep and announced to myself, "They meant to do that!" Not the sharpest tool in the shed, it took me years to realize the deliberate nature of that pitch.

The pitchers from my era enjoyed playing this 'Flip' game, one of them bats, the others field and flip the ball onto each other for accumulated points. I never had time or interest for such child's play, but pitchers on all teams seemed to enjoy the competition amongst themselves. Unlike any other team, the Red Sox pitchers would conduct their flip games, on the fair part of the foul line before their team's time to take the field. The home team takes batting practice first, and usually the starting lineup hits in groups of threes. I often hit in the first group, as I led off more than any other position in the batting order, although in 1983 I batted in all nine spots in the order. I may be the only major league player to have done that.

Anyway, after I hit, I went into the outfield to take ground balls off the live hitters, and one of my trademark talents was to go into foul ground on that sure double over the bag, barehand or backhand the would-be hit and throw the runner out at second. Somewhere on Youtube, there is a shot of Robin Yount succumbing to a 7-4 putout courtesy of yours truly. I asked the Sox pitchers who were often ten minutes ahead of their designated time, if they would wait before coming onto the field. They'd back off for a day, and then would be right back the next day, and this was repeated the next time they visited Arlington. I asked third base coach, Rich Donnelly to call over to the visitors' clubhouse to remind them not to come on the field before their time ... twice, and again, they were the only team to constantly violate the time slot.

So, the 'look out' warning before the hard sinker on my knee was to absolve themselves of blame from plate umpire, Ken Kaiser. Years later, I saw Stanley, then coaching in the New York Mets organization, in the Shea Stadium visitors dugout. Well, he saw me before I saw him. You know when you see someone, but you don't want to interact with that person, so you have that exaggerated time looking in one direction, so maybe the person won't know you're there. Yeah, we had that one. I guess I could have jumped in his face, but I didn't. Those are the times I wish I had the deportment of my brother, Thomas, who spent two tours of duty in the Marines ... and has muscles in his fingernails.

By today's standards, 1985 New York City was a dangerous locale; the 1384 people murdered, though representing a lull in numbers, was 66 less than the previous year and 198 less than the subsequent year, it still was over a thousand more murders than the 352 in 2015. A woman in the upper deck received a non-life threatening bullet wound in the leg at Yankee Stadium. The bullet was believed to have come from outside the stadium. There were constant fights in the stands; one evening, I counted seven fights, and those were just the ones I could see. Ushers seemed like some combination of hockey linesmen and trainers as they escorted combatant fans to the first aid room. It was an era in which fans constantly ran onto the field, those 8:05 starts on Friday nights, fueling the chances of liquid courage trespassing.

One night a guy staggered toward me in left and I started moonwalking back, he seemed harmless enough, but I was taking no chances. He left without incident, but there were those who would run around and try to juke the employees who were in charge of their removal. Sometimes the violators would be dropped on their faces as the workers all seemed to have spasms in their hands at the same time when descending the dugout steps. As a member of the Rangers, I had seen a beer bottle whiz past the face of teammate Johnny Grubb as he was chasing a ball in the corner, and was alarmed as a tequila bottle came from the second deck and landed about six feet from second baseman, Bump Wills. One day on the team bus back to the hotel, a male patron jumped from the ground to the hood and then quickly to the roof of the bus. The bus driver, taking no prisoners, sped up the bus and then slammed on the brakes, attempting to catapult the man off the roof to a hard landing. After all, he had no business on the roof of the bus.

This atmosphere was the backdrop of our workday, but considering all that was swirling around us, we lived a fairly harmonious existence, well, accept for Billy Martin and Ed Whitson. I have to admit to you right now that I was not in the bar the night of their infamous altercation in Baltimore, September 21 or 22, depending on how one charts late nights, that started in the bar and continued as they met again at the third floor elevator, ending up with Billy breaking his arm at some point during the altercations. I was in the bar the night before, and a non-player nearly got into a fight with Billy then. I watched long enough to see that there were no punches thrown, and then went back to my beverage.

I guess trouble often follows a reputation. I remember being on the top level of a bar in Arlington and a bar patron, whom I did not know, came up to me and pointed below to ask if that was Billy Martin. I confirmed that it was, and then this man proceeded to tell me that he was going to approach Billy with an offensive diatribe. I asked him for what purpose would he initiate such an insult, but before I could finish the question, he was off to the lower bar. Fortunately, he was picked off by members of Billy's coaching entourage, but it did get me to acknowledge how quickly things could get out of control in the Billy Martin traveling party.

Eddie Lee Whitson grew up in Erwin, Tennessee, sixteen miles south of Johnson City in the northeast part of the state. At the time of Eddie's youth, Erwin had a population of under five thousand, and it hasn't gotten much larger since. One of the town's noted events took place in 1916, when Mary the elephant, who had killed her handler in Kingsport, was hanged at the railroad yard by crane. The initial chain on the crane broke, but Mary's stay of execution was brief as a larger chain was brought in to finish the sentence. I know there is a segue here somewhere, but I just keep thinking about a blindfolded elephant smoking a cigarette.

Anyway, Whitson had parlayed a 14-8 record with a 3.24 earned run average with the San Diego Padres into a three-year, $800,000 per, contract with the Yankees. That guaranteed money was a good amount for a number two or three starter back in the day, and was more than twice the major league average salary of $368,998. Eddie gave up only ten earned runs in his first four starts, which was the good news. The bad news was that he finished without winning any of those outings. In his first outing at Fenway Park, he gave up only three earned runs, but nine overall and his error attributed to the unearned runs as he lasted only an inning and two-thirds. New York being New York, the snowball of blame rolled downhill at him and didn't seem to stop. Add to that, he found thumbtacks in his driveway, presumably left by some disgruntled fans, and the Smokey Mountains were a lot more appealing than Manhattan skyscrapers, or Bronx Borough buildings as the case may be.

Whitson won his first game in Texas on May 1st, didn't win his second game until June 19th in Baltimore, with a six-hit 10-0 shutout. He reeled off 8 wins in his next 9 decisions for a 10-7 record when he toed the rubber September 15th in the series finale of a four game set against the first place Toronto Blue Jays. The Jays lost the first game, but had taken the subsequent two games of the series to increase their lead over us to three and a half games. Matched up against former Yankee, Doyle Alexander, Whitson scattered three hits in the first two innings. However, in the 3rd, the first four batters reached, two scoring. Now with runners at second and third and Al Oliver at the plate, Billy Martin came to the mound with the hook. This early trip to the showers may have been the seed for the September 21st altercations, when coupled with Whitson being shelved from his next start in favor of Rich Bordi. Actually, what a compliment for Billy, who was never afraid to mix it up with his players, to have men half his age, 57 versus 30 years in this tale of the tape, wanting a large piece of him.

With such a productive offensive lineup there still has to be some rationality from one batter to the next to get the maximum benefit. Henderson, with a great on base percentage, is protected by Randolph, also with great on-base percentage, and he can take pitches to allow Rickey to steal bases while feeling comfortable batting deep into counts. Randolph followed by a great hitter like Mattingly, Mattingly protected by another great hitter in Winfield, and Winfield protected by a great RBI producer in Don Baylor, a league MVP as a Designated Hitter six years earlier with the Angels.

Now here comes the conundrum. There wasn't an easy, non-distinguishable drop-off from Baylor to whomever. In our right-handed hitting lineup, Baylor's presence most often dropped off to one William Amos Sample. True, his self-effacing nature notwithstanding, Sample was a solid hitter, but he didn't instill a lot of intrinsic fear into pitching staffs, unless it was the Angels, Red Sox or Brewers, the three teams that kept the 185 pound outfielder's ego afloat. Andre Robertson and Butch Wynegar were also solid candidates for protecting Baylor, but the point is, there was going to be some drop off whoever was providing the protection. Because I was not going to pinch-hit for Ken Griffey Sr., for the most part if I didn't start, I wasn't going to play.

I only played in 59 games as it was, 43 of them starts. Of the 43 starts, 28 times I batted behind Baylor, 17 times as the number 5 batter in order. Batting number 5 behind Baylor, did elevate the ego some, until one afternoon when I saw a tall right-handed reliever look at Groove (his nickname from the minor leagues, as in 'being in the groove' of hitting prowess), look at me in the on-deck circle and looked at Groove again at the plate. My heart sank, as I realized that Baylor was not going to get anything resembling a strike to hit. He's 6 ft. 2 in. and built like a University of Texas football player for which he was recruited. I'm 5 ft. 9 in. and, well, in all fairness, no one was built like Groove, who stood right on top of the plate. After the game I apologetically reported my observation to Groove, it was pathetic, my ego, well, what little I had left that year, was crushed. In one of the most considerate acts of teammate-ship I have ever experienced, probably sensing my whipped puppy-dog demeanor, the 15-year veteran waylaid my concerns by announcing, "The only walking I'm doing is to the dish!" Now, that's a teammate.

I was never teammates with this longtime Yankee, but I had always admired the seemingly quiet, dignified and classy way he carried himself in pinstripes during a number of lean years in the mid-1960s to the mid-1970s. As I, Roy White was converted from second base to left-field and we both finished our careers with batting averages in the lower .270s. Our careers intersected at the end of his fifteen years with the Yankees and the beginning of mine with Texas. I started to reach out to him as the sides retired one night in Arlington to tell him of my admiration, but just couldn't pull the trigger. I hardly ever conversed with visiting players before or during a game, and I sensed that he may not have either.

In 1985 Roy was working in a front office type position with the Yankees and was walking through the clubhouse, when I yelled for him to change his route and come by my stall. I announced under my breath, "Roy, I never had any role models, didn't believe in them for people I don't know, but I've always admired the quiet, dignified way you carried yourself in and out of the game." Roy, thought about it for a second or two, and with a delivery that rivals Orson Wells narrating portions of Citizen Kane, responded, "Yeah, right Bill, right!" Ha, I'd been harboring this compliment for quite a few years, finally got the opportunity to present it to the admired person, and he didn't believe me. Well, Roy possibly did believe me, but how is one supposed to react to a revelation like that? I remember when Bobby Meacham told me that he and his wife Gari, viewed my wife Debi and me as a model baseball couple for them. I knew Bobby was being sincere, but I felt slightly uncomfortable with the flattery, and responded, "C'mon Meach!"

There were a lot of admired people in and out of the Yankees clubhouse, but I don't think there was anyone more admired than longtime Yankees clubhouse attendant, Pete Sheehy. From 1927 to 1985, Pete bridged the years from Babe Ruth and Lou Gehrig to Don Mattingly and Dave Winfield, with DiMaggio, Dickey, Lazzeri, Rizzuto, Mantle, Berra, Stengel, McCarthy, Ford and Munson in between. I enjoy all types of history and baseball history in particular and he was a walking reservoir of baseball/Yankees history. Pete had been offered to write a book about the Yankees clubhouse, but it's not surprising that he turned down that offer with his respect of clubhouse sanctity. He found a willing listener in me, but I honestly don't remember a lot of specifics and what anecdotes of note he told me. I knew, as he did, that those would be taken to the grave with me, as he would take them to his grave. In fact, Pete would tell me these stories as I stayed late after games, with his hands covering his mouth as he spoke, still not quite trusting the carry of his whisper.

I don't think any of us knew just how sick Pete was; he was omnipresent, yet extremely quiet, and he left us quietly in August. A plaque was placed in the dugout which reads: "Pete" Sheehy, 1927-1985. Keeper of the Pinstripes. The name 'Pete' was in quotes as it wasn't his real name. He was given the nickname of Silent Pete early in his tenure by Fred Login, the clubhouse man who hired him as a teenager. Pete's given name was Michael Joseph Sheehy. I also later discovered that one of the secrets I thought I would have to take to my deathbed, Pete had already revealed, "Ruth never flushed the toilet."

I didn't think there was a large difference between the Dallas-Arlington-Ft. Worth media and their New York City brethren. The latter, Big Apple media had bigger numbers but the Metroplex, which covered the Arlington area was not exactly a one horse town. More numbers in New York might mean that a seemingly innocuous comment could appear in a more prominent section of the newspaper. And since there were some contentious negotiations between players and owners in 1985 resulting in a two-day labor impasse in August, one had to be a little more guarded than normal. I was so impressed with American League Players Association President, Don Baylor's ability to stay in the middle with his union-management comments, when there were some trap questions designed to trip him up.

Two and a half year old Ian is helping his Dad clean out his clubhouse stall on August 5th after a victory against the White Sox. The labor impasse would last only two days.

I was a "too staunch for my own good" union man. One day I counted three questions which, had I answered them, would have made headlines somewhere in the newspapers. I was also impressed with the way that Winfield responded to Steinbrenner when George wanted us to sign a voluntary drug testing policy edict which Commissioner, Peter Ueberroth was trying to negotiate unsuccessfully with the union's Executive Director, Don Fehr. The Winfield-Steinbrenner confrontation may have issued in the Howard Spira era, which proved to be a headache for both men. For more information about Spira and his relationship with Winfield and Steinbrenner and the subsequent consequences, I direct you to Luke O'Brien's Deadspin article, 'The Last Act of Notorious Howard Spira'.

I remember sitting at my clubhouse stall when I heard that Boss Steinbrenner labeled Winfield "Mr. May" in deference to Reggie Jackson's sobriquet, "Mr. October". Ouch! If we're playing "the dozens" (check your Urban Dictionary), advantage goes to the owner. All of New York, if not the world, remembers Reggie's three home runs on three consecutive pitches closing out Game 6 with a World Series win against the Dodgers in 1977. Four years later in his first season with the Yankees, Winfield had one single in 22 at bats in New York's six game World Series loss to the Dodgers. It would take the 6 ft. 6 in. slugger eleven years to erase the memory of 1981. In 1992, Winfield capped off a World Series victory with the Toronto Blue Jays over the Atlanta Braves. In the top of the eleventh inning, he hit a two-run double over the third base bag, off a Charlie Leibrandt change-up. The Jays held on in the bottom of the inning for the organization's first World Series title, a title they would repeat the following year.

In the Yankees clubhouse in 1985, the aforementioned Steinbrenner's criticism of Winfield seemed to cast a short-term pall over our preparation for the games. Maybe in 1977-78 when the Yankees won their first two World Series under Steinbrenner, criticism would evoke a 'We'll show him attitude', but Willie Randolph and Ron Guidry were the only holdovers from that era, and the disparagement just didn't seem to spark the engine. Different era, different people, different sensitivities and no newspaper strike that coincided with the Yankees erasing a 14 game deficit against the Red Sox in 1978. Thank goodness the Boss didn't single me out for my lack of clutch-hitting. I would have hated to have to wear the sobriquet, "Mr. March" for the remainder of my career.

Back to the Fourth Estate. The only area I thought the New York media exceeded the Texas media in negativity was in assigning blame for failures and miscues. They had that questioning down to a science and with the complexities of the relationship between George and Billy and the players, with the media scurrying around trying to capture anything that was headline worthy, there potentially was a lot of blame to assign. I told one New York sportswriter that he was lucky, he never had to search for a story, stories materialized right before his eyes.

Let me fast forward fifteen years to give you one example of assigning blame that stunned me. I was in my first year of working for MLB.com, Major League Baseball's Internet website, covering the post-season in 2001. After Mark Grace's leadoff single representing the tying run in the bottom of the ninth, Mariano Rivera failed to close out a game seven World Series victory when he threw wide to second on Damian Miller's sacrifice bunt. He did get the force at third on Jay Bell's sacrifice bunt attempt, but gave up the lead on Tony Womack's double down the right-field line that drew the infield in. That hit allowed Luis Gonzalez' jammed shot to reach the outfield grass for the World Series winning hit.

One of the first questions posed to Rivera at his clubhouse stall, was something like this, not an exact quote, "With the backdrop of the Alomar home run in Cleveland, have you established a pattern of failure in big games?" I was paralyzed. I had never heard a question so pointed and potentially inciting after a game of this magnitude. Actually, I had never covered a game of this magnitude and I could not have answered that question without some kind of emotional response. As I recall, Mariano answered the question explaining that his wide throw to second was the catalyst for the inning, but he wasn't going to beat himself up more than the situation would allow. Mariano had the aforementioned blown save in Game 4 in 1997 that would have closed out the Divisional Series for the Yankees in Cleveland. Game 5 also went to the Indians, completing the come from behind series win. Since that blown save, Mariano had amassed 23 post-season saves and a World Series MVP. If someone of this magnitude, who had four World Series rings in his possession at that time, could be pinned down for blame, then the assigning of blame in 1985 with no post-season appearances, even with the understanding that there was no wild card back then, could be harsh.

A little side note before I go back to 1985, back at the Chelsea section of Manhattan studios of MLB.com, we interviewed The Amazing Kreskin. The mentalist, a Montclair, New Jersey native and lifelong Yankees fan was promoting *The Amazing Kreskin's Future With The Stars*, one of his now twenty books. At the end of the interview, I asked him how he sees the Yankees performing that year. He felt that they would perform extremely well, it would be a great year by most teams' standards, but there was something that kept him from saying that they would win it all, and you could see in his face that there was some kind of fly in the ointment that had him hesitate. After watching the ninth inning unfold in Phoenix, I thought that the Amazing Kreskin is indeed 'amazing'.

My two big games of Yankees blame came in the same week, the second week of September. The first one was in Milwaukee, in the ninth inning of a tied game, facing young promising southpaw, Teddy Higuera. I was 1 for 4 with a run scored, but failed to get a bunt down in a game that was now tied at 3, in the bottom of the ninth. Mike Felder and Paul Molitor singled off of reliever Rich Bordi. Dave Righetti was brought in to face Cecil Cooper after Randy Ready sacrificed the runners over to second and third. I guess Brewers manager, George Bamberger wanted to stay out of the double play with the sacrifice. There was a base open for Cooper, with left-handed hitting Dion James, who had pinch-run for Ted Simmons in the eighth, scheduled to bat next, but the decision was to go after Cooper, who hit a line drive down the left-field line towards my right shoulder as I'm running after it.

At this point there is a lot of information to process in a couple of seconds. I know I cannot throw out the speedy Mike Felder no matter how I catch the ball; diving or on my feet, with momentum carrying me away from the play. Should I let the ball go, hoping that it will carry into foul ground? Should I make a diving catch and hope that Felder pulls a hamstring watching me make the catch before easily trotting home with the winning run? As I leaned to make the final play on the ball slicing away from me, I noticed that my left foot had crossed the foul line and I attempted to pull my glove back away from the ball just in case the ball was traveling from fair to foul grounds, thus allowing it to land foul. I thought the ball landed foul, but in all honestly, I wasn't completely sure, so there was no need in debating the fair call of third base umpire, Vic Voltaggio, who, before making a decision, had to deal with as much stimuli as I, the least of which is the way the outfield sloped down significantly and unevenly from the infield.

Before the next game, with our return to Yankee Stadium, reporter/anchor, Sal Marchiano interviewed me about that play. I tried the best I could to say that the ball landed foul, but that it was a difficult call for Voltaggio, who is a good umpire. I'm guessing Sal saw the replay and it appeared to land foul? Ha, I don't know, I still haven't seen the game winning hit more than thirty years later.

My second play of blame happened three days later on September 14th. It was Game 3 of an extremely important four game series in the Bronx against the first place Blue Jays. The first two games were split and with the game tied at 2 in the top of the sixth, our closer Dave Righetti replaces Rich Bordi with one out and one on. Billy Martin was a believer that often the most crucial time of the game is not necessarily in the ninth inning when the team's closer almost always comes in to nail down the victory, but that the most crucial time could be any time before that, and it was the sixth inning for this contest. I doubt if anyone seriously argues the logic of this especially with the resume of Billy Martin; to me it's a matter of choice somewhat similar to managers who have the pitcher batting eighth in the batting order.

Anyway, you'll have to ask Righetti, who has had so much success in San Francisco as their pitching coach, what he thinks about that decision. I think I know, but for whatever reason on this night, Dave did not retire any of the four batters he faced, the key blow being a Rance Mulliniks run scoring double over my head in left. Now, I played a deeper outfield than most, some of it was philosophy as I felt that a single in front of me was not going to hurt as much as a double over me, but I also charged the line drives in front of me well, thus cutting off many cheap singles. If Mulliniks hits a ball over my head, then he put a very good swing on the pitch, but as I was running after the ball, knowing that I wasn't going to catch it, the thought crossed my mind, that I was going to get blamed for not making this catch.

With the 7-4 loss came the sobering realization that we were not going to gain ground on the Blue Jays and actually could leave the series two games further behind than when we started, which eventually happened. For this failure, George had blamed Billy, but Billy hadn't heard the critique before he left the ballpark, and was ready to absolve himself of blame by the next day. Now I understand that in the blame game, it is more prudent to blame the spot playing outfielder as opposed to the team's shutdown closer, I get that, but I still wasn't quite ready to accept more than my share of the blame. So, when Billy was looking to apply the blame torch to this Billy, I didn't accept it wholeheartedly; in fact, I didn't accept it at all.

"Did you guys see Sample running after that line drive last night? He looked like a dog chasing a Frisbee!" The 'dog chasing the Frisbee' line originated from Peter Gammons, who was in town covering the series. I had heard the quote before and had to wear it as I knew I wasn't an exceptionally smooth looking outfielder. Billy looked for affirmation around the small group gathered, but more importantly, he looked for acceptance of the criticism, and that would have to come from me.

I thought of Ron Hassey, who could easily roll with the criticism when Billy second-guessed his pitch selection, finding that happy medium of placating Billy while not totally agreeing with the assessment. I wish I could have been more like Ron, if I could have found a small window to allow everyone to be happy, I would have, but I couldn't. I like to laugh, will poke fun at myself and have readily accepted blame, but I just couldn't do anything but return a look that officially landed me in the doghouse with a two-foot leash.

Just a few days after my banishment to the Chateau Bow-Wow, one of the most interesting developments of the season happened in Detroit. Right-handed Tigers' starter, Juan Berenguer, retired only one of six batters he faced in the top of the first, and when he walked Don Baylor with the bases loaded to force in the second run of the game, Sparky 'Captain Hook' Anderson, gave meaning to the moniker earned as a manager in Cincinnati and replaced Berenguer with left-hander, Mickey Mahler.

Mahler's first batter is Mike Pagliarulo. Mike's a great storyteller, so at this point I will briefly defer to him, "While on deck, Lou (Piniella) came out to me and handed me a helmet with the right-handed hitter's ear flap. I asked, 'what the hell is this?' He said Billy wants you to hit right-handed. I answered and said 'no'. He said if you don't, you'll have to come out of the game. Well, I got up to the plate right-handed and completely had no idea what to do. I mean if I had practiced or had some heads up, I would have had a chance, but it was thrown at me while I was on deck and I just froze and couldn't get the bat off my shoulder." The result, a strikeout.

To at least one player on the bench, Mike's right-handed at bats were some of those surreal moments when life swirls around you, and you can't quite make sense of it all. In this situation, 'at bats' is plural, because there were two more Mahler-Pagliarulo match-ups this evening, ending with the same outcome, the last time with runners at second and third, with two outs, and first base open, in the sixth.

For those of us who didn't know, and that was just about everyone, word did get to us that Pags was a switch-hitter his first season in the minors, playing short-season A ball in Oneonta, New York. Okay, I'll accept that a player from the state of Massachusetts talented enough to play at a major collegiate powerhouse like the University of Miami may have some impressive skills, but not batting from the right side four years removed from his last swing on that side of the plate. It turns out that Mike had been practicing his right-handed swing. Well, that's not quite accurate. Again, let me have Mr. Pagliarulo tell the rest of the story.

"I was at the field early one day and I believe Marty Bystrom was pitching a simulated game. Billy came to see Bystrom throw and saw me hit. There was a left-handed hitter, yet they needed a right-handed one. As luck would have it, after grounding out, I hit the ball well. I got a base hit to right field and then a one-hopper off the wall in right-center. Billy went nuts and said, 'What the hell are you doing? You should be switch-hitting!' I explained that the reason I got to the major leagues was due to the fact that I gave up hitting right-handed."

So there is the backstory. Whether it was an experiment or the chance to catch lightning in a bottle, it lasted for three plate appearances. With two out in the top of the ninth, trailing by three, facing Tigers' closer Willie Hernandez, Mike was spared another right-handed at bat by pinch-hitting third baseman-shortstop, right-handed hitting, Andre Robertson, who ended the game by fouling out. After chasing Berenguer in the first inning, the seventh spot in the order options this evening was to have Pagliarulo bat left-handed, Andre Robertson or Dale Berra batting from their natural right-handed side or Pagliarulo batting from his four year removed right side, with one day of batting practice from a simulated game three to four weeks prior ... and it was the latter that we went with on this night. More than three decades later, the surprised third baseman, if not quite absorbing blame, has internalized responsibility, "I felt terrible that I didn't come through." Pags was a Billy Martin favorite. You can understand why.

Oh, I just remembered another play of blame, and this one preceded the previous two; maybe I was building up to the doghouse. On July 9th, at Yankee Stadium in the middle of a three-game series with the Kansas City Royals, Hal McRae hooked a Ron Guidry offering down the left field line. Similar to the way we defensed Ken Singleton of the Orioles, we bunched McRae in the outfield, meaning as it might sound, the off-fielders played closer to the center-fielder. I don't recall having flow charts, or positioning arrow sheets, and this was long before computer programming, so we must have played defense on intuition, common sense or memory.

Anyway, I'm in left field and I've got a long way to run. Lonnie Smith at second base is going to score easily and George Brett at first is near second base before the ball lands; he scampers back to first base easily if I catch it, and if I don't and the ball kicks away from me, then he scores easily. The ball is headed for the part of the stands that has curvature similar to a hockey rink, and a baseball has the same action as a puck being shot around the boards as a defenseman tries to clear the puck out of the zone. I get to the curvature and attempt to jam my body against the padding as the ball and I reach a certain spot at the same time.

In the end, I kept the ball from hooking around the sideboards, but I admit, it didn't look like I was auditioning for Swan Lake while doing so. I did keep McRae at second with a two-run double instead of a two-run triple, so I felt that I was moderately successful. Well, evidently someone above field level didn't think so, and before the game the following day, I was summoned to left field to practice taking line drives off of the curvature in left field. 'Eye in the Sky' coach, Doug Holmquist drew the assignment of hitting me balls with the fungo bat, as we tried to replicate game situations, but similar to playing the ball off The Wall or the Green Monster at Fenway, it's nearly impossible to recreate what will happen during a game. The tin of the Green Monster doesn't have the same thickness throughout the structure, so the bounce you get pre-game could be a lot less or more than when the bounces count on the stat sheets.

Well, Doug and I did the best we could, we never could quite get the McRae line drive that sent us out there in the first place. It was a good workout for me, heck, I was starting in only a fourth of the games, so any attempt to keep game sharpness was a help in my view. Rationalization aside, Doug, a Billy Martin favorite and as I understood as a minor league manager was a fair, yet tough taskmaster, called a halt to this exercise as I think we both realized that this was as much punitive as it was instructional, and the punishment had been served. By the way, not that I had anything on the offensive side of the ledger to affect the outcome, but the game in question, my teammates defeated the Royals, 6-4.

How about a short incident of blame that didn't involve me? Highly regarded White Sox pitching coach, Don Cooper, had an outstanding curveball as an active player. He heads the short list of New York Institute of Technology Baseball collegians to make it to the major leagues, and was drafted by the Yankees in the 17th round in 1978, subsequently making it to the majors as a Minnesota Twin in 1981. By 1985 the 6 ft. 1 in. right-hander, returned to the big leagues with the Yankees after spending a year in the minors and another year in Triple-A after his trade to the Yankees in March of 1984.

On June 2nd of 1985, Cooper had been twelve days between appearances when he came out of the bullpen with four Mariners already having scored, and runners on first and third with one out. He retired the next two batters to keep the Mariners' lead at 4-2. Cooper retired the Mariners in order in the top of the fourth. Not bad at all for someone who hadn't pitched in nearly two weeks. Well, Don's good fortune ran out in the fifth inning. Domingo Ramos hit the first offering, a fastball, deep to right-centerfield for a home run, it was the first and only homer that season for the native of Santiago, Dominican Republic. Phil Bradley followed with a double, Ivan Calderon moved Bradley to third and Alvin Davis singled Bradley home, in what would be a Mariners 7-6 victory at the stadium in the Bronx. The RBI single to Davis, would be the last pitch Cooper would throw in the major leagues, banished from the fraternity, with an explanation I heard that included, "You know you don't throw a Latin player a first pitch fastball!"

For a very competitive team, with a manager who was no stranger to altercations, oddly there were no bench-clearing brawls in 1985. I felt that even less competitive teams would walk into a fight or two as the summer heats up. Talented, skilled, often Type-A personalities in pressure situations are going to have margins cross from time to time and very seldom do people play up to fifty percent of another's margin;

when the margins cross, confrontations can happen, bodies may get thrown.

Now, to let you know that I'm not necessarily an advocate of this type of behavior, I have not been in a fight with punches thrown by at least two combatants since the fourth grade, and my adversary then, Ronald Crockett, won that one. It was a decision, as opposed to a knockout, but I knew I was losing the fight and was glad when it was over. I challenged Crockett to a rematch the following school year, his protection buddies transferring schools coincided with my ability to complete two pull-ups. I was certain that we'd have a different outcome this time, but he declined. I did issue the challenge while he was at the urinal, which might have had some bearing on his decision.

The following year, a kid named Glenn, who resided at the Baptist Children's Home, demanded that I show up for one of those, 'you can't escape from' fights. Hands were to be exchanged at the designated field for such disagreements, a block and a half from our elementary school shortly after the school's final bell. A combination of fear and adrenalin inhabited my body as the pugilists made their ways to the center stage. And then for no apparent reason, the crowd that had gathered around in a loosely shaped circle began to disband. The fight was called off as if a boxing promoter had determined it would not be economically viable, or more viable in a different venue on another day. I'm guessing one of the teachers had found out about it and would be there to mete out punishment for the combatants. It would take me until my first year in professional ball to have a similar confrontation and this time it was much more spontaneous.

In Short-season A-ball or Rookie ball in Sarasota, playing against the Cubs' affiliate, first round draft pick

Herman Segelke, with the swagger of a high school pitcher who had never had his fastball hit, drilled me in the ribs with a pitch. That in itself did not raise my ire, though to put something on the right-hander's microscopic earned run average (2.20 at season's end), I did promptly steal second, and scored as left-handed hitting outfielder, Greg Jemison rifled a ball into center-field. As I crossed the plate I looked back to see if Jemison had advanced to second on the throw to the plate and I went flying backwards. As I gathered myself, I saw Mr. 'Seventh Pick Overall in the Draft' strut towards the mound as if he hadn't shouldered into an unsuspecting me. In fact, he didn't acknowledge that any physical contact had been made.

I charged after the guy, throwing punches wildly. I knew nothing about rubbing my ribs with my elbows while throwing punches and it wouldn't have mattered anyway, as he was 6 ft. 4 in. and backing up, and as we have established I'm 5 ft. 9 in. My manager Joe Klein, grabbed me from behind, most likely to keep me from hurting myself, as my errant swings had a greater chance of hitting me in a boomerang with the air, than landing on my intended target.

I'll ask your indulgence for one other fight memory, and that does not even include saving teammate Jim Sundberg from getting viciously blindsided in Kansas City one night, after Mike Smithson hit Amos Otis in the head, and Amos released the bat twice toward the mound in his next plate appearance.

This brawl, and it was a doozy, took place in Arlington on June 22, 1983. In a battle for first place against the Angels, trailing the visitors by a game and a half, our All-Star pitcher, Rick Honeycutt stranded two Angels in the top of the first. In the bottom of the inning, Wayne

Tolleson singled to left and one out later, advanced to second on a Buddy Bell walk. Angels' second baseman, Bobby Grich called for a pick-off play at second in which he'd traditionally drop his knee in front of the third base side of the bag, not allowing the baserunner access to getting back to the bag safely if he went back diving hands first. Players, especially young players who didn't know the league, were instructed to go back to the bag standing up if they could, or feet first to discourage the dropping of the knee.

On this evening, Tolleson went back to the bag standing up and inadvertently bumped Grich in the face. They briefly exchanged philosophies on how the game should be played. Evidently, they had near polar opposite views of game etiquette, because when Grich called for the pick-off play again in advance of a pitch to the plate from southpaw Bill Travers, he made no attempt catch the throw, which went into center-field.

Instead, Grich started punching Tolleson, who at 5 ft. 8 in., is six inches shorter than his second base counterpart. Now, Wayne is not void of quickness and athletic ability. He was an All-Southern Conference wide receiver at Western Carolina University and he attempted to tackle and lift Grich as the feud began in earnest. The team in the field has the initial advantage in bench clearing brawls; they already have nine players with a head start toward the point or points of altercations.

I felt as if I was running in slow motion trying to get out to the second base area to protect my fearless teammate. When I got there, I noticed that a member of the light gray suited Angels, was pummeling the back of the head of one of my white suited Rangers with his forearms, or at least that's how it appeared to me. I grabbed the offending player in a Half Nelson wrestling hold. I only know this because Bret Lewis, now a local sports anchor at the CBS affiliate KDFW, announced to the television audience that was indeed my grappling hold.

I picked the Angels player off the pile and slammed him back from whence I had lifted him. He tried to wrestle away from my grip and I helped him with his momentum upwards, and when he reached the apex of his ascension, I gave him a little extra lift and slammed him back into the pile. At this point I have to admit, I was feeling good about my leverage and strength, but before I could think about my next move, someone made the move for me. I felt a hand on the back of my collar, the hand lifted me up, I could feel my feet leave the ground, and rolled me onto my back. I looked up to see and feel Popeye forearms on my chest. In a fraction of a second, I went from 'go for bad' to just being in a bad situation. Before I had time to determine how many punches in the face I'd have to eat before freeing myself of Popeye's grasp, Mr. Forearms said, "That'll be enough!"

—'Yeah, this gratuitous violence really isn't necessary is it?' my mind thought but mouth did not speak. Playing the role of Popeye Forearms was first base coach and previous longtime Angels' second baseman, Bobby Knoop. Eleven years later when I was an Angels' radio broadcaster, I reminded Bobby, who was still in the same capacity with the club, about how strong he was in the incident. He seemed almost sheepish about his actions, but I reminded him that his role as a coach was to break up fights, and he fulfilled the role very efficiently.

Playing the role of Angels' player temporarily getting mugged by Rangers' outfielder was 6 ft. 1 in. right-hander Byron McLaughlin. Byron had an outstanding change-up. I rolled over on it more times than I care to remember, both in the Pacific Coast League and in the majors. Fortunately neither he nor his change-up were hurt in the brawl, at least I don't think so as he finished the season with a win on September 27th, his last outing in the majors. I did conclude that grabbing a pitcher in a fight was the best way to protect myself from getting jumped by other opposing players. The chances of me falling on the pitcher's throwing shoulder is too great, and that possibility acts as a deterrent. The fall is, ahem, unintentional of course, ahem. Pardon me, having trouble clearing my throat today.

As I mentioned earlier, no bench-clearing brawls in 1985; even the closest potential player versus player confrontation ended without incident. Red Sox right-handed reliever, Steve Crawford unhinged Don Baylor with a head high fastball. Baylor took a step or two towards the 6 ft. 5 in. Crawford while pointing his finger in warning, but went no farther. For a player who led the league in getting hit by the pitch eight times, including this year, wearing no arm-guard protection, the reaction caught me a bit off-guard.

Well, Groove, like most of us, wasn't thrilled by pitches at the head, but I remembered my first week in the majors, playing in Anaheim. Reggie Cleveland of the Rangers threw Baylor one of those similar decapitating pitches, batter goes down, helmet goes flying. I thought to myself, 'They play for keeps up here!' Later in the at bat, Groove takes a Cleveland slider and hits a homer to left-centerfield. At that point, I realized that the players on the varsity got here for a reason. So, it's with this backdrop that I watched the Crawford pitch and subsequent reaction. Remember a few pages ago when Groove soothed my bruised ego about batting behind him in the order? Well, I repaid his consideration by telling my teammate that there was nothing between him and that country-strong, white boy on the mound but air and opportunity. "You just weren't sure you could take him."

Groove managed a chuckle towards his teammate whose elevator may not stop on all of the floors.

EYE CHART ZONES

I honestly felt that the umpiring in the minor leagues was better than it was in the majors. There were some calls in the big leagues, especially behind the plate, that were hard for me to imagine someone with a trained eye missing. I think I had a progressive attitude towards our arbiters, that we were all part of the entertainment package, and I respected the difficulty of their job and could in no part handle what they do.

I still have regrets about a call I missed as a young adult, umpiring behind the plate of a Senior League game. The throw came to the plate for a bases loaded force play and I forgot the force was on, anticipated a tag that was not needed, and called the runner safe, when he was out by a good half step. The catcher rightfully complained, I realized my mistake, but was so caught off-guard that I tried to defend my blown call. The catcher cut me some slack and let it go. I wish I could properly identify him now as I'd really like to apologize. I know, the incident is over forty years old, let it go Billy.

Speaking of apologies, I'd also like to offer one to Dave Phillips. It was hard to find a more competent, conscientious umpire as Davey, but one day I snapped at him as if I didn't respect him at all. It was at Fenway in 1984 and he gave Bob Stanley a high sinker strike for strike two. I didn't say anything, but when he gave Stanley a low, below the knees strike three, I lost it. I was having the worst year of my career, but I'd like to be person enough not to use that as an excuse. I told Davey, "You can give him this one (indicating the high pitch) or that one (indicating the low pitch), but you can't give him both!"

The next day as I was coming out of the third base side of the dugout toward left-field for the bottom of the first, Davey met me to apologize for the blown call, noting that the way (Rick) Cerone caught the ball, threw off his judgment. Seldom if ever had an umpire admitted a mistake to me, and yet I didn't want to hear the rationale and brushed by Davey, as I was still steamed from the previous night. I think everyone has a desire for a do-over, especially in a game like baseball, as one moment can alter the course of history. That is a do-over of deportment that I'd like to replay. Wish I had handled this situation more professionally, especially toward a person I admired.

However, before your eyes get too moist regarding the umpires, I have some situations that my deportment was just where I wanted it to be. On April 18th of my first full year in 1979, with the scored tied at 3, one out and Bump Wills in scoring position at second, Cleveland starter Eric Wilkins missed low and outside with a slider then missed on the subsequent pitch with another slider that was caught in the dirt. At neither pitch did I offer a swing, but both were called strikes, the second of which was strike three.

I would say that plate umpire, Ted Hendry, missed the pitches badly, but that would not be entirely true, as actually the two missed pitches were initially called strikes by catcher, Gary Alexander. Now, I don't know if Hendry confused me with a player who gave him a hard time in the Caribbean Winter Leagues, I hear that happens from time to time, but I reacted just to the calls that should be much better arbitrated in a highly select profession like Major League Baseball, and went off on him. I said all that I had to say while walking away as Hendry followed me with his eyes and some of his body to the dugout. I was in the clear until I bounced my helmet over the dugout roof, and received my heave-ho, the first and only ejection of my career.

As I collected my tools and walked toward the clubhouse, I was met by Richie Zisk, who again played the avuncular role similar to my first day in the majors the previous season. He explained how selfish a play my ejection was; it left the team a player short for manager Pat Corrales' late game moves. And sure enough I left Pat a batter short, as I would have been in the game to face left-handed reliever Sid Monge, who picked up the victory in a 6-4 Rangers loss. At the point of my ejection, I had reached base twice and scored both times. Monge struck out Larvell Blanks, who was pinch-hitting for Johnny Grubb in the ninth. I could have saved two moves had I not been ejected.

Because Zisk's warnings had come to fruition in that contest, I had trouble expressing myself after that day, though I wish I hadn't taken that situation so much to heart. I'm not sure umpires appreciated my passive-aggressive nature in expressing my disgust with their decisions, like smirking or rolling my eyes. I had let my consternation build with John Shulock, which had started when he called a 3-2, two-out, bases loaded, Jack

Billingham fastball crossing the plate area somewhere in the middle of the left-handers' batters box; strike three.

I was stunned, no one in the minor leagues had missed a pitch by such a margin. After that, I made note of Shulock's positioning at the start of the series. If he started a three-game series at third, I would exhale a sigh of relief since he would not umpire behind the plate. If he started anywhere else, I seemed to always be subject to a pitch off of the plate being called 'strike three' in a crucial situation. A few years of this and I had tired of plate trepidation whenever the former Minnesota Twins farmhand was working behind the plate. I had concluded that the reason he and I didn't see eye to eye, might be one of DNA, ethnicity or ancestral origin, and this analysis coincided with seeing Shulock walking across the field before a spring training game in which he was an umpire. I headed right to him. I was going to get some answers and if I didn't like the responses, he and I were going to the ground, and I was giving away about seven inches and thirty pounds.

"John, you've been screwing me ever since I got into the league!" (Though insert a word that starts with the sixth letter of the alphabet in place of screwing).

John chuckled, "I've been getting you too?!"

Talk about defusing an argument with the quick release of balloon air. We chatted for a couple of minutes more with the congeniality of high school athletic teammates and I never had a problem with John after that. Yeah, right, how much earlier could I have had this conversation with him?

I didn't realize that I had a problem with tall, angular umpire, Bill Haller until September 19, 1981, when as with Ted Hendry a couple of years earlier, the veteran umpire missed strikes two and three badly, with strike three being a 'strike' only in bowling. After the missed strike two, I looked back as a pet might who doesn't quite understand what is happening, but on strike three, I knew I was being screwed. I don't know why I'm the target of his suspension of arbiter ethics, but I know the action is definitive and with forethought.

I dropped the bat at the plate as I walked to our first base side dugout, and that may have been my all-time favorite passive-aggressive move. I don't know if Haller was trying to bait me into an argument so he could toss me, but it's hard to miss pitches that badly and not elicit a reaction, whether intentionally missed or not. The dropping of the bat registered my disgust with the calls to the paying crowd and showed up the umpire at the same time, though falling just a little shy of getting an ejection. Well, the game within a game was not quite over, as Haller told catcher Jim Sundberg to tell Sample, "He'd better be swinging!"

I'll admit at times Bill, I'm a little slow, but I was never quite that slow to think that I had the ultimate advantage in this situation. My last plate appearance of the evening had me swinging at Bob Veselic's first pitch-fastball that was centimeters away from my thumbs. I hit the ball so poorly that it never reached any of the fielders and had backspin like a golf shot. I can still feel the sense of relief and enjoyment now as I did some thirty-five years ago when I safely crossed first base; poetic justice I thought. Oh, and we won the game 6-0.

BILLY SAMPLE

INTERNALIZED PROTECTION

Lately there has been a lot of talk about slides at second base. In the aftermath of the late and across-the-bag slide of Chase Utley on a spinning Ruben Tejada, breaking the shortstop's right leg during Game 2 of the 2015 National League Championship Series, legislation is now in place (Rule 6.01j) that essentially eliminates the 'take out' slide. What fun is that? I enjoyed the challenge of trying to break up a double play. No longer could I put an instep on the foot of a leaping, super quick Julio Cruz? Rangers second baseman Rougned Odor took umbrage with Jose Bautista's slide after the Blue Jays slugger went hunting for a middle infielder after taking a 96 mph purpose pitch fastball in the ribs? Mr. Odor let me introduce you to Don Baylor, Hal McRae, Dave Parker, Pete Rose, Bill Madlock, Kirk Gibson and company. And the ensuing altercation would last longer than one punch.

Oh, I understand the safety issues of protecting the valued workforce, but as an old-timer I often enjoyed the rank and file drawing up the unwritten rules. Here are a couple of more examples of players legislating the game, involving me.

In 1979, I attempted to break up a double play at second base by roll blocking Angels' shortstop Bert Campaneris; not a slide and roll, but a straight roll block. I didn't realize that the slide was illegal until second base umpire Ken Kaiser indicated that not only was I out for the illegal slide, but the batter was out as well. The smallish Campaneris was not averse to taking matters into his own hands. Some of you may still remember Bert flinging his bat at Tigers' pitcher, Lerrin LaGrow, during Game 2 of the 1972 American League Championship Series, after LaGrow hit Campaneris on the ankle with a pitch. Campy had two hits and two stolen bases at the time of the incident. On this day in Arlington, Bert ever so deftly lifted his spikes over my rolling ankles, causing a 340 degree cut that took a couple of days to heal.

Four years later on a steal attempt at Yankee Stadium, I took Bert's glove off during the slide and stolen base. My rationale for taking his glove off was that he tried to hold his position as long as he could before covering the bag, and the ball, his glove and my feet all arrived at the same time. My feet arrived with maximum force. While Bert was counting to see if he still had five fingers on his left hand, I did offer, with questionable sincerity, a "Sorry about that, you okay?" It was a Saturday NBC *Game of the Week*. If the slide had appeared to be too egregious, they probably would have shown the replay a few times in a one-run contest. I simply think the 41 year-old Campaneris was too late in covering the bag, ahem. That's my story and I'm sticking to it.

The only other time I remember sliding in such a manner that took the middle fielder's glove off his hand did have some malice aforethought. It happened in Arlington in 1984, but the situation started a week before in

Milwaukee. On a head-first stolen base attempt slide, second baseman Jim Gantner, blocked the bag with his knee and lower body and tagged me out from a one-hopped throw from catcher Ted Simmons. I looked up at second base umpire Drew Coble as if to ask, "Is he allowed to do that?" Drew looked past me as he ran to his position before the next at bat. "Well, I guess Gantner is allowed to do that."

The back end of the home and home series was just a week later. Jim Sundberg, the very popular former Rangers' catcher, also returned to Arlington at this time for the first time as a member of the Brewers after an off-season trade. Over the years as teammates, I had seen the 6-time Gold Glover throw out a plethora of would-be base stealers and I didn't want to be added to the total. It was no secret that I was going to run and he was going to throw, and he threw a laser to second. I could sense after my first few steps that the play was going to be very close and I also knew that after what happened in Milwaukee, I was going to slide feet first ... and with authority. If Gantner wanted to block the base with his body, he would do so at his own peril.

My slide took his glove off with the ball in it. As Gantner checked his hand for skin lost, I offered my mea culpa to shortstop Robin Yount, who gave me a 'that's baseball' shoulder shrug. Bottom line is that I was in scoring position and Gantner would have to think twice about dropping his body in front of the bag again. Remember when I said that Sundberg was very popular in Arlington? Well, Jim was also extremely popular with the sportswriters and those were the days when the active sportswriters took turns as official scorers. I was not credited with a stolen base, but a 'caught stealing' ... bummer! The outcome was worse for Gantner; not only did he get spikes jammed up against his hand, but he was also charged with an error for not holding onto the ball.

So it doesn't always sound like I'm seeking retribution on middle infielders, let me tell you a story where I showed my compassionate side. White Sox infielder Jim Morrison was working on his footwork around the second base bag a couple of hours before the game. As a passing observer, I thought he looked a bit stiff. And he really looked unpolished when I came bearing down on him during the game a few hours later, to break up a double play. He was taking a throw from third and had no idea how quickly I was on top of him. I was into my slide at his feet a second before he had the ball. I would have torn up his knee(s), and players didn't recover from ACL surgeries thirty-five years ago as they do today. Come to think of it, how often does one hear about ACL injuries in baseball? They are that rare. Anyway, I just didn't have the heart or competitive edge to hurt him. To this day, I suffer from insomnia wondering what I should have done in situations like this.

I'll finish the book with one of my favorite stories about a favorite of many, who has been battling his health over the last few years. I was taking pre-game batting practice in the cage on the field in Arlington on one of those 100 degree days, which could be the norm for any day in the summer. We were hosting the Orioles and Oriole great Brooks Robinson, now a television analyst, was making the rounds gathering information to add to his insight for the broadcast that evening.

He greets me and says something very flattering about my game. I rolled my eyes at him while wondering if the Texas heat has reduced his mental capacities. Evidently he wasn't broadcasting those games in which Mike Flanagan, Sammy Stewart or Storm Davis were painting every pitch on my hands or two inches off the outside corner for strikes. I finished another round of swings and Brooks is at it again with the compliments. Now, having one of the game's greats bestowing compliments that I received from no one else is quite an honor, but I honestly couldn't think of anything special I did against Baltimore to warrant his glowing review of my game. Maybe the Texas heat was getting to me too, because I had heard enough.

"Brooks, I have such high status and am so popular, that my grandmother-in-law can't find baseball cards of me!"

Well, you know where this is going. The next time we face the Orioles in Arlington, Brooks walks up and hands me a rubber-banded stack of about fifty of my baseball cards. Now, this is an incredible gesture if Joe 'Green Fly' fan presents me with this gift. But this is Brooks 'Bleeping' Robinson taking the time to acquire those baseball cards. Decades later, I still can't tell or write this story without a lump in my throat or a couple of tears in my eyes.

I trust you have enjoyed many of my experiences in baseball. I can admit now that I'm not even in the top whatever percentile of baseball players who can entertain an audience with reflections of their experiences in and out of the game. I have been connected to baseball in some capacity for over thirty years and yet I still tear up in laughter whenever I reconnect with former teammates and opponents while hearing them pontificate about their views of the past, present and future. To enhance your vicarious living through these people who have mastered, to the highest degree, a certain set of special skills, I would encourage you to attend card shows, book signings, Alumni functions, and if you can afford it or someone can afford it for you; attend a fantasy camp or two. The former jocks get paid to interact with you on and off the field. Now, you may have to participate in some late night libations, but it'll be a small price to pay for the camaraderie. Remember to take a couple of aspirin beforehand.

A New Beginning

The veterans, Pete Van Wieren, Ernie Johnson Sr., and Skip Caray treated the broadcast rookie well in 1988. The Braves lost 106 games and with my monotone voice that was not a good combination for late innings enthusiasm.

ABOUT THE AUTHOR

After playing in the majors from 1978-86 with the Texas Rangers, New York Yankees and Atlanta Braves, Billy broadcasted with the Braves, Seattle Mariners and the California Angels, as well as ESPN and CBS Radio Sports. The Salem, VA native has also been published in Sports Illustrated and the New York Times. His screenplay for the irreverent baseball clubhouse comedy *Reunion 108*, took top honors at the Hoboken Film Festival (in 2011). He continues his attempt to warrant the honor of Most Versatile from his Andrew Lewis High School class of 1973.

Made in the USA
San Bernardino, CA
20 October 2016